Dealing with the Past
in Security Sector Reform

Alexander Mayer-Rieckh

Published by
Ubiquity Press Ltd.
6 Osborn Street, Unit 2N
London E1 6TD

First published 2013

Editors: Alan Bryden & Heiner Hänggi
Production: Yury Korobovsky
Copy editor: Cherry Ekins

This book was originally published by the Geneva Centre for the Democratic Control of Armed Forces (DCAF), an international foundation whose mission is to assist the international community in pursuing good governance and reform of the security sector. The title transferred to Ubiquity Press when the series moved to an open access platform. The full text of this book was peer reviewed according to the original publisher's policy at the time. The original ISBN for this title was 978-92-9222-285-7.

SSR Papers is a flagship DCAF publication series intended to contribute innovative thinking on important themes and approaches relating to security sector reform (SSR) in the broader context of security sector governance (SSG). Papers provide original and provocative analysis on topics that are directly linked to the challenges of a governance-driven security sector reform agenda. SSR Papers are intended for researchers, policy-makers and practitioners involved in this field.

The views expressed are those of the author(s) alone and do not in any way reflect the views of the institutions referred to or represented within this paper.

Suggested citation:
Mayer-Rieckh, A. 2018. *Dealing with the Past in Security Sector Reform.* London: Ubiquity Press. DOI: https://doi.org/10.5334/bbu. License: CC-BY 4.0

Contents

INTRODUCTION

Security sector reform (SSR) and transitional justice, or dealing with the past (DwP) as it is also called,[1] are among the key challenges confronting societies emerging from conflict or authoritarian rule. In such contexts, SSR and transitional justice processes commonly occur alongside each other, involve some of the same domestic actors and often receive support from the same multilateral or bilateral partners.[2] However, the two fields rarely interact in either theory or practice.[3] Commonly, the other field is not referred to, discussed at a level of generality that can be void of meaning, misunderstood or even seen as an impediment to achieving one's own goals. Conversations between the two fields are often deadlocked around ill-framed debates about peace versus justice.

At best, the debate is framed around interactions between otherwise separate fields. Erin Mobekk, for instance, discusses various transitional justice measures and examines how they interact with SSR, both positively and negatively.[4] Paul van Zyl argues that transitional justice measures such as criminal prosecutions, truth commissions and vetting programmes can greatly enhance SSR processes.[5] For Tim Murithi, SSR can contribute to transitional justice in that it corrects the role of security institutions after conflict or authoritarian rule. Equally, transitional justice can complement SSR because it helps to overcome a culture of impunity. At the same time, he identifies tensions between SSR and transitional justice measures that may arise as a consequence of criminal prosecutions and truth-seeking efforts.[6]

This paper argues that SSR and transitional justice are not separate fields but intrinsically linked with each other in societies in which serious abuses occurred. On the one hand, DwP depends on SSR to provide justice in times of transition. Justice after mass abuse encompasses not only seeking and acknowledging the truth about what happened, criminally prosecuting at least the most serious perpetrators and repairing the consequences of those violations in symbolic and material ways, but also making sure that the atrocities do not happen again in the future. Security actors are often responsible for many of the most serious abuses, either by not preventing them or by directly perpetrating them. Reforming the security sector is, therefore, one of the principal ways to ensure the non-recurrence of abuses.

On the other hand, SSR can achieve its own goal of building an effective and accountable security sector more successfully when it learns from transitional justice and integrates some of its methods. Proactively dealing with an abusive past makes the security sector more accountable, inclusive and legitimate, which in turn represent conditions for its effectiveness. Acknowledging the abusive past also helps the security sector to turn the page and commit with more determination to a future based on democracy and the rule of law, thus facilitating the SSR process itself. Ultimately, the kinship between DwP and SSR relates to the fact that the democratic rule of law is a goal shared by both fields.

Understanding some of the intrinsic linkages between the two fields and recognizing their interdependencies can help to overcome the artificial divides. While this paper does not ignore the potential tensions that can arise between DwP and SSR efforts, particularly in the short term, it aims to show that both fields can benefit from and enrich each other. The author hopes that the paper could stimulate a conversation that has only just begun.

Methodologically, the paper starts with an analysis of the concepts of SSR and transitional justice in recent literature and policy documents, particularly in reports of the UN Secretary-General. On this basis, it proposes a richer understanding of DwP and SSR that acknowledges the correlations between the two concepts. These correlations are further developed in terms of their practical applications. The validity of this position is tested in two case studies, namely Bosnia and Herzegovina and Nepal: in the first, the abusive past was partially taken into account; in the second, the past was ignored. The methodological limitations of this approach relate mostly to practical constraints. In most previous SSR processes, little attention has been paid to the legacy of past abuses, which limits the cases that can be used to test the assumptions of this paper.

The paper has four main parts: two conceptual sections and two empirical sections based on case studies. The first section describes the concepts of SSR and transitional justice and discusses how they are related. It shows that, in recent literature, their relationship is usually understood in competitive terms. But DwP depends on SSR to provide justice. Moreover, a failure to deal with the abusive legacy of a security sector often prolongs the exclusion from this sector of victims and marginalized groups, perpetuates a culture of impunity and extends the climate of distrust in the security sector. The second section proposes, therefore, three groups of measures that are particularly important to deal with an abusive legacy in SSR: promoting the inclusion of victims of serious abuse and other marginalized groups in the SSR process and the security sector; holistically strengthening accountability for past, present and future abuses; and proactively enhancing the legitimacy of security institutions. The remaining two sections describe and analyse two cases to test the assumptions put forward in the first two sections. The third section looks at police reform and development efforts in Bosnia and Herzegovina between 1995 and 2002. Efforts to deal with the abusive legacy of the police in Bosnia and Herzegovina have been resisted, but also helped to move the police reform process forward and made the police more accountable, inclusive and trustworthy. As a result, the performance of the police improved. The fourth section analyses SSR efforts in Nepal after its ten-year armed conflict came to an end in 2006. The refusal to deal with the abusive legacy of Nepal's security sector has created a risk that impunity could become the norm of the future, extended the exclusion of marginalized population groups from the security sector and further undermined the legitimacy of the sector. The conclusion sums up the paper's findings and provides several policy recommendations.

THE RELATIONSHIP BETWEEN SECURITY SECTOR REFORM AND TRANSITIONAL JUSTICE

This section describes in general terms the concepts of transitional justice and SSR, and examines how the relationship between the two is commonly understood. It is argued that a competitive understanding of this relationship is insufficient. The two fields do not only affect each other but are intrinsically interlinked.

Preliminary descriptions

Two of the most accepted definitions of SSR are those articulated by the United Nations (UN) and the Development Assistance Committee of the Organisation for Economic Co-operation and Development (OECD DAC). The UN definition of SSR refers to "a process of assessment, review and implementation as well as monitoring and evaluation led by national authorities that has as its goal the enhancement of effective and accountable security for the State and its people without discrimination and with full respect for human rights and the rule of law".[7] The OECD DAC defines SSR as a locally owned process to increase a country's ability "to meet the range of security and justice challenges … in a manner consistent with democratic norms, and sound principles of governance and the rule of law".[8] These two definitions are not identical. Among others, the OECD uses the term "security system", which is broader than the UN's concept of the security sector. But these differences are of little relevance for the purposes of this paper. In both these and other definitions, three elements are fundamental: first, SSR is a *locally owned* and locally led process; second, SSR aims at ensuring that security and justice providers deliver *effective* services that meet the people's needs; and third, SSR aims at ensuring that security and justice providers are *accountable* to the state and its people, operating within a framework of good governance, rule of law and respect for human rights.[9]

The notion of "security sector reform" originated in the late 1990s as an explicit development concept that "intellectually justified the development community's venture into security-related activities".[10] In 1999 the then UK secretary of state for international development, Clare Short, referred to security as an "essential prerequisite for sustainable development", and to "bloated, secretive, repressive, undemocratic and poorly structured security sectors" as principal obstacles to poverty reduction.[11]

As a result, SSR began to be seen as a significant condition for sustainable development. According to the United Nations, "security, human rights and development are interdependent and mutually reinforcing conditions for sustainable peace"; SSR therefore aims to develop "effective, inclusive and accountable security institutions so as to contribute to international peace and security, sustainable development and the enjoyment of human rights for all".[12] Along similar lines, the OECD DAC states that "development and security are inextricably linked", advocates a "developmental approach" to SSR and emphasizes its "critical importance for supporting sustainable development".[13] The World Bank devoted its 2011 World Development Report to the subject of conflict, security and development. It found that no fragile or conflict-affected low-income country had so far achieved a single Millennium Development Goal, and that poverty rates were 20 percentage points higher in countries affected by repeated cycles of violence. In analysing the causes of violence and development shortfalls, the report found that "strengthening legitimate institutions and governance to provide citizen security, justice, and jobs is crucial to break cycles of violence".[14]

The notion of "transitional justice" emerged in the late 1980s to mid-1990s within the international human rights movement.[15] Up to the mid-1980s, "naming and shaming" of repressive regimes had been both the main approach and the central aim of the human rights community, since accountability for violations committed by repressive regimes was largely unattainable. However, in response to the ending of repressive regimes in Latin America in the 1980s, the human rights community had to adapt to the new challenges of transitions from authoritarianism to democracy. Rather than just denouncing violations, it had to develop practical approaches to dealing with legacies of past abuse in often-fragile political contexts. An important effort in the context of the United Nations to compile these measures resulted, in 1997, in the formulation of UN principles to combat impunity.[16] The package of measures described in these principles and applied in transitional contexts to dealing with abusive legacies began to be referred to as "transitional justice". The United Nations defines transitional justice as "the full range of processes and mechanisms associated with a society's attempts to come to terms with a legacy of large-scale past abuses, in order to ensure accountability, serve justice and achieve reconciliation".[17] According to the United Nations, these mechanisms comprise, in particular, criminal prosecutions, truth-telling efforts, reparations and institutional reforms, including vetting.[18]

The *prosecution* of genocide, crimes against humanity, war crimes and other international crimes is an essential component of transitional justice. Trials are not only a fundamental demand of victims but also send a strong signal that such crimes will not be tolerated under the rule of law. But the large-scale nature of these atrocities often means that not all perpetrators can be prosecuted. In general, effective prosecution strategies focus on the planners and organizers of such crimes.[19] Through *reparations*, governments recognize and take steps to address the harm suffered by victims. Reparation initiatives usually have material elements (such as compensation payments) and symbolic aspects (such as public apologies).[20] *Truth commissions* or other truth-telling efforts are means to investigate, report on and acknowledge the systematic abuses that have occurred. Truth commission reports usually also include recommendations to address the root causes of the abuses.[21] *Institutional reforms* of abusive institutions, particularly in the security and justice sectors, help to dismantle the structural machinery of abuses and legitimize these institutions to prevent the recurrence of abuses.[22] These measures of transitional justice should not be thought of as isolated pieces, but as mutually reinforcing parts of a comprehensive transitional justice effort. Together, they stand a better chance of meeting the rights of victims, promoting reconciliation and facilitating the transition to a democracy based on the rule of law.[23]

Transitional justice has to be distinguished from notions such as "justice reform", "judicial reform", "administration of justice" or "justice sector reform".[24] Whereas transitional justice focuses on dealing with legacies of massive past abuses, the latter aim at building a functioning, independent and accountable justice system that enables people to obtain judicial remedies.[25] Transitional justice efforts usually involve the establishment of *ad hoc* mechanisms such as truth commissions, special courts, reparation programmes or vetting commissions to deal with the extraordinary challenges of massive and systemic past abuse. Justice reform efforts, on the other hand, focus on developing a permanent judicial system able to provide judicial remedies under ordinary circumstances. Another related term used in this context is "access to justice". Initiatives to provide access to justice empower and assist marginalized population groups to use formal and informal mechanisms to seek justice.[26] The notions of "traditional justice" and "informal justice" refer to customary, non-statutory justice mechanisms that may operate alongside state justice systems,[27] and are also used in the context of transitional justice.[28]

Some have criticized the use of the term transitional justice for its narrowness, because it does not capture the full range of all of its attending processes.[29] Mistakenly, transitional justice is sometimes thought to cover criminal justice processes only. Sometimes it is also misunderstood to be a minor, "transitional" form of justice rather than the provision of justice in times of transition. The alternative notion of "dealing with the past" has been proposed and is also used in the literature. Its origins can be traced back to the German words *Vergangenheitsbewältigung* or *Geschichtsaufarbeitung*, which may be translated as "dealing with", "coping with", "treating", "confronting" or "overcoming" the past. The term "dealing with the past" has been introduced by historians rather than by human rights activists;[30] in recent years it has been promoted particularly in Switzerland,[31] and is closely associated with the fight against impunity in the aftermath of serious human rights abuses, which is also at the origins of the transitional justice concept.[32] While transitional justice remains the far more commonly used term and conveys more clearly the normative dimension of confronting an abusive legacy, the notion of DwP represents an acceptable alternative that relates more directly to the experiences and activities concerned.

In terms of context, this paper looks at societies in which serious abuses occurred but were not punished, and which are in transition, or strive to transition, to a democracy based on the rule of law. By serious abuses the paper refers especially to serious crimes for which international law places an obligation on states either to extradite or to prosecute. They include, in particular, genocide, crimes against humanity, extrajudicial executions, enforced disappearance, torture and slavery.[33] These abuses usually took place during authoritarian rule or an armed conflict. Pablo de Greiff describes this type of context as a "very imperfect world ... [that is] characterised not just by the massive and systematic violation of norms, but also by the fact that there are huge and predictable costs associated with the very effort to enforce compliance".[34]

SSR in general is not limited to societies that emerge from conflict or authoritarian rule and are confronted with legacies of serious abuse; it is also applied in development contexts without histories of serious abuse where there is a need to improve the effectiveness and accountability of the security sector. In these contexts, there is no abusive past to deal with and the question of transitional justice does not arise. This paper does not cover these cases, but focuses on contexts in which serious abuses took place and hence in which both SSR and DwP have a crucial role to play.[35]

A competitive status quo

In societies emerging from conflict or authoritarian rule, practices of SSR and DwP regularly occur alongside each other and are often supported by the same domestic and international actors. Nevertheless, the fields rarely interact, either in practice or in theory. In relevant writings, the other field is often not referred to, discussed at a level of generality that can be void of meaning or even misunderstood. Conversations between the two fields are commonly deadlocked around an ill-framed peace versus justice debate. In the SSR literature, transitional justice is regularly meshed together or even confused with judicial reform. For instance, the OECD DAC *Handbook on SSR* discusses transitional justice in its section on justice reform and puts it among justice reform's "particular features of post-conflict settings".[36] Along similar lines, in an important article on the concept of SSR, Michael Brzoska states that "there is a danger that traditional security sector reform activities might be crowded out by judicial sector reform activities such as transitional justice and access to justice which are highly worthy in themselves but have little to do with the provision of physical security in a narrow sense".[37] Brzoska not only seems to misunderstand transitional justice as a subset of judicial reform, but is also concerned that SSR risks being marginalized by transitional justice. In other examples, the SSR literature ignores transitional justice altogether. For instance, the UK Department for International Development (DFID), which has been and continues to be at the forefront of developing and promoting the concept of SSR, makes no reference to transitional justice in a recent and comprehensive publication on SSR.[38] The report of the UN Secretary-General on SSR does not discuss or reference transitional justice.[39]

The UN Secretary-General's report on the rule of law and transitional justice provides only a fleeting reference to SSR and does not explain it or link it to or distinguish it in any detail from the core concepts of the rule of law, justice and transitional justice that are defined and discussed in the report.[40] The report devotes an entire section to vetting the public sector to screen out abusive officials, but fails to situate vetting in its broader context of SSR or other areas of public sector reform. In a practice paper on justice and accountability, DFID provides an overview of how justice systems contribute to accountability. The paper makes a brief reference to transitional justice, which is defined as a means to pursue accountability for the worst abuses in periods of transition. It limits transitional justice to criminal prosecutions, truth and reconciliation processes, and reparations and restitution, but does not include or refer to SSR (or institutional reform more broadly) as efforts to prevent the recurrence of abuses.[41]

SSR and transitional justice experts and practitioners not only frequently fail to understand each other, but significant cultural and institutional barriers also persist between the two communities. Transitional justice actors generally come from and see their origins in the human rights community, which is often perceived by security actors as soft, lofty and unreasonably idealistic. The SSR community, on the other hand, continues to be dominated by former uniformed personnel and political actors, who are often perceived as too narrowly focused on operational concerns and overly realist by transitional justice and human rights actors. Few are those who attempt to cross the line and engage in constructive conversations with the other community, and they are often viewed with suspicion in their own community. The Center for the Study of Violence and Reconciliation in South

Africa and the International Center for Transitional Justice (ICTJ) are examples of organizations engaging directly with both fields. However, when the ICTJ faced a financial crisis in 2008–2009, its SSR programme was among the first to be discontinued.

In transitional settings, DwP and SSR frequently share some of the same historical catalysts (such as access to resources or ethnic conflicts), face some of the same political barriers to reform and target some of the same institutions in their programmes. At the same time, the immediate aims of SSR and transitional justice may diverge and their programmes can get in each other's way during implementation. For instance, calls to hold perpetrators to account for atrocities committed in the past may have a destabilizing effect on the security sector; or the removal of security officials may negatively affect the sector's capacity to provide effective services. Frequently, SSR and DwP programmes also compete for the same resources provided by bilateral and multilateral donors. For instance, funding is frequently provided to reform and develop the security sector but little funding is available for reparation programmes, and the victims of abuses suffer additional harm.

Both SSR and transitional justice will, then, be genuinely interested to pre-empt negative repercussions of the other's practices on their own programmes. Hence the unavoidable interactions between the two fields remain at the level of competition and establish a relationship that is determined by defensive postures on both sides.

Transitional justice's dependence on security sector reform

But from a transitional justice perspective, this cannot be the last word. SSR is not just a different field with which DwP inevitably interacts and competes in transitional settings. Transitional justice depends on SSR to ensure that the abuses which occurred in the past do not happen again in the future.

Transitional justice is frequently misunderstood to be based on no more than a narrow, moralist notion of accountability, and sometimes even reduced to criminal accountability for past abuses. But such an understanding misses out on an important dimension of justice in transitional societies. For one, accountability by itself is not just backward-looking but provides for forward-looking political justifications, in that it reaffirms the equal validity of basic norms.[42] Criminal justice denies "the implicit claim of superiority made by the criminal's behaviour through a sentence that is meant to reaffirm the importance of norms that grant equal rights to all".[43] In addition, the concept of accountability by itself cannot fully capture the various aims that transitional justice pursues. Justice in the aftermath of conflict or authoritarian rule cannot be reduced to measures of accountability for past abuses, but must, at the same time, prevent their recurrence. For instance, if we were to live through a "perfect" transition in which all abusers are criminally prosecuted, all past abuses are documented and acknowledged, and all victims are repaired, but did not at the same time stop the continuation of the same abuses and take steps to prevent them from happening again in the future, we would not do justice. Preventing recurrence of abuses is a significant aspect of dealing with their legacy, and hence of DwP. This is why the UN principles to combat impunity introduce, in addition to the rights to know, to justice and to reparations, a fourth category: the guarantees of non-recurrence "to ensure that the victims do not again have to endure violations that harm their dignity".[44]

Efforts to prevent recurrence in transitions may include a broad range of measures, including peacekeeping, DDR programmes, legislative reforms, economic development, educational reforms and others.[45] Critical among these are institutional reforms, including SSR. More often than not, it is security agencies, unofficial armed groups, private military and security companies and other security actors that have committed the most serious abuses in the past and represent the greatest threat to a transition to the democratic rule of law; or ineffective security agencies have been unable or unwilling to prevent others from committing atrocities. Moreover, security sector oversight and management actors have, for various reasons, not provided effective governance of security providers. Reforming the security sector and building a society's "capacity to manage conflict without violence", then, is a central concern of transitional justice.[46] SSR can also enable other transitional justice measures. For instance, vetting of security institutions could remove spoilers that obstructed other transitional justice measures; or, more generally, the building of effective prosecution and police services could enable and accelerate criminal prosecutions. Therefore DwP is – or should be – interested in ensuring that SSR complements rather than obstructs criminal prosecutions, truth-seeking and reparations.

Transitional justice without SSR to prevent recurrence can only be incomplete justice. This is why definitions of transitional justice include institutional reforms, particularly in the security and justice sectors, as one of the key measures. For instance, the United Nations includes institutional reform, vetting and dismissals in its definition of transitional justice.[47] The article on transitional justice in the *Encyclopedia of Genocide and Crimes Against Humanity* refers to "reforming a wide spectrum of abusive state institutions (such as security services, police, or military) in an attempt to prevent future violations" as one of the key strategies.[48] Along similar lines, the ICTJ emphasizes the need to approach transitional justice holistically and lists institutional reforms of abusive state institutions as one of four core measures. The purpose of such reforms is to "dismantle ... the structural machinery of abuses and prevent recurrence of serious human rights abuses and impunity".[49]

The effects of an abusive past on the security sector

So far, this paper has argued that transitional justice needs SSR as a complementary justice measure to prevent the recurrence of abuses. But is the inverse also true? Does SSR need DwP? In fact, except for recognizing that SSR can complement other transitional justice measures, would it not be advisable to keep the two fields apart because the institutional cultures, operational challenges and reform techniques have little in common and often require different skill sets? For instance, establishing a truth commission requires a wholly different set of skills and knowledge than reforming an intelligence service. While incompetent interference in the other field must be avoided, this paper proposes that SSR can actually benefit from a closer examination of both the normative framework of and the practices applied in transitional justice, and learn from transitional justice how to deal with legacies of an abusive past. Such an examination does not lead to a new or entirely different concept of SSR, but can enrich common understandings and provide supplementary tools to conduct SSR more effectively in societies emerging from conflict or authoritarian rule.

The developmental origin of SSR is the reason for its largely forward-looking agenda. Commonly, SSR starts with an analysis of the existing deficits of a security sector, and from there develops a reform agenda aiming to build an effective and accountable sector: "SSR is meant to turn a dysfunctional security sector into a functional one."[50] Thus common approaches to SSR generally cover two major categories of activities:

"measures aimed at rebuilding, restructuring and reforming the security apparatus and the relevant justice institutions" and "measures aimed at strengthening civilian management and democratic oversight of the security apparatus and the relevant justice institutions".[51] Within this context, the past matters in so far as it led to a deficient present state of the security sector that SSR aims to overcome; but beyond the identification of existing capacity deficits, the effects of abusive histories of security actors are often not given much thought. For instance, in a paper discussing the particular challenges of SSR in conflict-ridden societies, Heiner Hänggi introduces a third category of SSR activities: measures aimed at addressing the specific legacies of violent conflict. But when he describes these measures in more detail he distinguishes "standard reform activities" from "SSR-related activities such as DDR of former combatants, curbing the proliferation of small arms, mine action, transitional justice and the establishment of the rule of law".[52] While these activities are part of what Hänggi calls security sector reconstruction, they are not part of SSR *per se* but SSR-*related*: they complement the standard SSR agenda in post-conflict settings. The reform agenda rarely addresses directly the abusive histories of security actors. In SSR practice, dealing with abusive legacies is often overlooked, or sometimes perceived as a distraction from SSR or, even worse, an impediment to effective reform.

An exploration of the use of the concepts "prevention" and "accountability" in the reports of the UN Secretary-General on SSR and on the rule of law and transitional justice can further clarify the different positions taken towards abusive histories of security actors. "Accountability" is a central concept in the report on SSR[53] – the term and variations of it appear 18 times. Mostly it appears in phrases such as "effective and accountable security institutions" or "effective and accountable security sector", and refers to one of the two fundamental goals of SSR: to build a security sector that is accountable to the state and its people. Accountability in the report thus largely concerns the legal framework, and discipline, oversight, management and governance mechanisms that ensure the legitimate use of force and financial propriety.[54] It is accountability *to laws and structures* that are to be established to ensure good governance and full respect for human rights in the future. "Accountability" is also a key concept in the UN Secretary-General's report on the rule of law and transitional justice.[55] Again, the term and variations thereof appear 18 times. Where the term is discussed in the context of the rule of law, it is used along the lines of the report on SSR;[56] but it takes on a somewhat different meaning when it is used in the context of transitional justice. Here, the term does not refer to structures to ensure future accountability but to accountability for past abuses. It is accountability *for specific past abusive acts* and relates to obtaining justice in redressing such abuses. This is reflected in phrases such as "accountability for the past", "accountability for perpetrators", "accountability for serious violations" and "hold violators to account".[57] Whereas accountability in the SSR context is forward-looking and refers to systems, it is backward-looking in the transitional justice context and refers to individual acts.

The term "prevention" and variations of it appear seven times in each report. In the UN Secretary-General's report on SSR, the concept refers to generally preventing future crimes (e.g. "crime prevention", "violence-prevention initiatives" and "prevention of sexual and other forms of gender-based violence and organised crime")[58] or preventing countries from relapsing – in general, unspecific terms – into conflict.[59] The report on the rule of law and transitional justice often uses the term "prevention" along similar lines.[60] However, where it is used in the particular context of transitional justice, the concept takes on a more nuanced meaning and refers to preventing recurrence of specific past abuses (e.g. "putting an end to such violations and preventing their recurrence").[61] Similarly, the UN principles to combat impunity refer to guarantees of non-recurrence.[62] Both SSR and transitional justice aim to prevent conflict and abuse. But SSR refers to the prevention of conflict and crimes generally, and makes unspecific allusions to the past, while transitional justice aims to prevent the *recurrence* of specific abuses that happened in the past.

Both transitional justice and SSR aim to contribute to building a democracy based on the rule of law.[63] Both share a common concern for a peaceful, secure and just future. But they contribute differently to achieving this goal. SSR focuses on building an effective and accountable security sector, which is an essential aspect of democratic rule of law. Transitional justice, on the other hand, is specifically concerned with the direct consequences of an abusive past, the "spill-over effects" into the present and future,[64] and aims to redress this abusive legacy by means of various measures in order to contribute to reconciliation and democratization.[65] In principle, the type of measures used and the institutions targeted are open-ended in transitional justice, as long as they deal with the abusive past.

The respective contributions of SSR and DwP to building a democracy based on the rule of law are not – as they are commonly understood – parallel approaches each contributing in its own way to building a democratic rule of law, but each has subjects of a different nature that relate to each other. The subject of SSR is institutional: the security sector that is to be reformed. The subject of DwP is a situation: the legacy of an abusive past that is to be redressed. As a result, DwP and SSR can overlap and contribute to each other in contexts in which a security sector is confronted with a legacy of human rights abuse.

Due to its largely forward-looking agenda, common approaches to SSR tend to pay less attention to the effects of an abusive past on the security sector. But a failure to address abusive histories of security actors manifests itself in different ways and leads to various deficits that negatively affect the functioning of the sector. The following paragraphs discuss three common manifestations of a failure to address an abusive legacy and their effects on the security sector: exclusion, impunity and distrust. This analysis will help to understand how DwP can directly contribute to SSR.

One way in which legacies of serious abuse often manifest themselves is a continued *exclusion* of certain social groups from the security sector. Conflicts and authoritarian rule commonly lead to a marginalization of certain groups and generate a large number of victims who are excluded from the political community. In the security sector, the exclusion manifests itself in the removal of marginalized groups from positions in security institutions, or barring their employment or promotion; a failure to meet the security and justice needs of victims and other marginalized groups; and the continuation of direct abuses targeting these groups. Continued exclusion after the end of conflict or authoritarian rule can be the intended effect of a sustained pursuit of conflict-related aims or the unintended outcome of neglecting the plight of victims and other marginalized groups. As a result of continued exclusion, the security sector is not in a position to provide security effectively and fairly to a significant segment of the population, and SSR programmes which ignore this exclusion are not able to deliver on the overall objectives to build an effective and accountable security sector. The first case study on policing in Bosnia and Herzegovina illustrates how police services that are dominated by a majority are not trusted by minorities, and may be used actively to pursue illegitimate aims.

Another way in which an abusive legacy manifests itself in the security sector is the existence and continued employment of a significant number of personnel who have committed serious abuses in the past. Not holding them accountable not only perpetuates a culture of *impunity* but also conveys a general sense that security officials can bend the law to escape accountability and might be able to do so again in the future. Continued impunity affects the trustworthiness of the security sector and undermines the rule of law. Confidence in the rule of law will not be enhanced if impunity rather than the law is the rule for those in power.

The continued presence of abusive security personnel who are not held accountable often also perpetuates the existence of criminal structures and networks within which individuals committed criminal acts in the past and which provide opportunities for continued abuse.[66] During the period of conflict or authoritarian rule, the members of such networks cooperated in order to protect themselves, to pursue particular political or military objectives or to ensure illegal gains. Membership of a network can be based on ethnicity, a political or religious objective, clan membership or a purely criminal purpose, among other reasons. Such networks are usually not confined to one security institution but comprise members of different institutions, representatives of political groups and members of non-official armed groups, as well as ordinary criminals. If abusive security personnel remain in place and are not held accountable, such networks often continue to exist and to be used for abuses, and loyalties towards a network are frequently stronger than the commitment of security personnel to their institutions and legal responsibilities. These networks frequently aim to influence appointments and promotions in order to create dependencies and place their members in positions of power; they also tend to interfere inappropriately in the operations of security institutions. Moreover, such networks are generally not interested in SSR because it would make it more complicated for them to operate. As a result, not only is a security institution ineffective and biased in the delivery of its services, but also its officials may remain involved in abuses that go unpunished and may even block SSR efforts. A culture of impunity is perpetuated. Again, the case study on police reform in Bosnia and Herzegovina provides an example of relationships and collusion between the police and criminal networks.

Legacies of serious abuse also express themselves in a fundamental *crisis of trust* in the security sector. Security institutions depend for their effective functioning on the trust of the people. Without trust, the people are unlikely to report crimes, are not likely to turn to the police and the courts to resolve their conflicts, and will hardly seek the assistance of the police and other agencies for their security. Involvement in serious abuses undermines the legitimacy of security institutions. Their trustworthiness is further undermined by a continued presence of security personnel who were involved in abuses in the past. If the public face of institutions remains associated with abusive officials and if lawbreakers are entrusted with enforcing the law, the people will come to understand that the law is not applied equally and that security officials are above the law. This trust deficit reduces the effectiveness of security institutions. Moreover, once trust is lost, it is hard to regain.[67] The people, particularly those who suffered violence and abuse, will find it hard to gain trust in security institutions that do not signal a clear turning away from past abusive practices but continue to operate with the same personnel who were involved in abuses, keep the same organizational structures that were instrumental in inflicting abuse, display the same signs and insignia that have become symbols of abuse, and use the same buildings and locations in which abuses were inflicted.

To sum up, ignoring legacies of past abuses can affect in various ways the functioning of security institutions. Particularly, it can continue the exclusion of marginalized groups, prolong a culture of impunity and perpetuate the existence of criminal networks that provide opportunities for further abuse, thereby reducing the effectiveness of the security sector. Ignoring abusive legacies can also undermine trust in the sector and erode emerging confidence in the rule of law. Moreover, abusive officials usually have little interest in supporting reform, as it may expose their past failures, remove their sources of income and power, and oppose the goals they pursued during the conflict or authoritarian rule. As a result, the failure to deal with legacies of past abuse can derail the SSR process itself.

APPROACHES TO DEALING WITH THE PAST IN SECURITY SECTOR REFORM

We have seen that past abuses are not just bygone, but present in their legacies. Abusive histories of security institutions have various detrimental effects on the effective functioning of these institutions and may also render SSR more difficult. Ignoring the effects of abusive histories or pretending that they do not exist does not eliminate them. Only by dealing with abusive histories can their effects be mitigated. This section begins to explore the question of how SSR can deal with the past, and argues that three groups of measures are particularly important to deal with an abusive legacy: SSR should promote the inclusion of all people, but especially of victims and other marginalized groups, holistically strengthen accountability for past, present and future abuses, and proactively enhance the legitimacy of security institutions.

Promoting inclusion

Common approaches to SSR emphasize the need for it to be shaped and driven by local actors, based on an assessment of the security needs of the people and focused on improving delivery of security services. SSR should be "people-centred" and "locally owned".[68] In periods of conflict or authoritarian rule, security actors are usually there to protect the regime and its allies. Therefore, in the aftermath of serious abuses, particular efforts should be made to reverse the process of excluding victims of abuse and other marginalized groups and reaccept them in the political community.

Their inclusion will help ensure that the security sector actually services the needs of all people; restore the status and sense of full citizenship for victims and other marginalized groups; and promote the credibility of the SSR process and of the security sector itself.

The inclusion of victims and other marginalized groups can be advanced, in particular, by paying attention to four areas: promoting their participation in SSR processes; enhancing their representation in security institutions; establishing structures in the security sector that meet their specific security needs; and their empowerment as citizens. These four areas are described in more detail in the following paragraphs.

Subjects of violence and abuse have a clearer understanding of what needs to be reformed. Their involvement in SSR will be critical to ensure trust in the process, and help to move from a regime-centred to a people-centred understanding of security. SSR processes should not be a prerogative of security actors. Particularly in the aftermath of serious abuses, the involvement of victims and other marginalized people helps to endorse a people-centred understanding of security. Promoting their *participation* in SSR processes can be done, for instance, in the following ways.

- Organizing broad-based population surveys on justice and security needs, with a particular focus on the needs of victims of systematic abuse and other marginalized groups. For instance, in 2004–2005 the Afghanistan Independent Human Rights Commission conducted national consultations to propose a strategy on addressing the abuses of the past. The consultations showed that Afghans viewed justice as a prerequisite for sustainable peace and perceived a close link between the absence of accountability and the lack of security.[69] In another example, in 2008 several international non-governmental organizations (NGOs) conducted a survey of 2,620 individuals in areas most affected by conflict in the eastern Democratic Republic of the Congo. The survey sought to assess exposure to violence among the population; understand the priorities and needs of Congolese civilians affected by the conflicts; and capture attitudes about peace, social reconstruction and transitional justice mechanisms. It found, among other things, that peace and security were the two top priorities of the population. Moreover, a strong majority of the population believed that accountability for past abuses was necessary to achieve peace.[70]

- Linking SSR processes with truth-seeking efforts that allow victims to express how security actors abused them, which represents the basis for recommendations on SSR needs by a truth commission or other truth-seeking body. The Moroccan Equity and Reconciliation Commission, for instance, examined more than 22,000 applications for consideration and held public hearings with victims throughout Morocco in 2004–2005. In its final report the commission made, among other things, recommendations to strengthen governance and oversight of Morocco's security sector.[71]
- Designing SSR assessments in a way that ensures consultations with victims and other marginalized groups. Along these lines, the OECD *Handbook on SSR* states that the perceptions of marginalized and impoverished communities provide the baseline data for planning and measuring effective SSR interventions.[72]

Adequate representation of victims and other marginalized groups, as well as of women, among the staff members across all ranks of security institutions provides for internal checks and balances within these institutions, helps to overcome the pursuit of single-group interests and improves the overall distribution of power and resources. Equal access to public office is also an internationally guaranteed human right.[73] Moreover, a more representative security institution will better understand the concerns of all population groups because its representatives will speak their languages, comprehend their cultures and appreciate their traditions. As a result, the institution will better serve and respond to the needs of all groups – including those who were previously victimized, marginalized or excluded – and respect them as rights-bearing citizens.[74] In Bosnia and Herzegovina, for instance, a dedicated programme was established in 1996 to increase the number of minority officers in the various police services. In Sierra Leone the police established a gender unit in 2012 to ensure the implementation and monitoring of gender-related policies and make the police a more gender-responsive and equal opportunity institution.[75]

The establishment of structures that meet the specific security needs of victims and other marginalized groups after the end of authoritarian rule or a conflict helps stop further abuses and restore these people's status as full citizens. Such structures include the following, among others.

- Dedicated mechanisms to respond to gender-based violence, such as the inclusion of female investigators in cases of such violence.[76] For instance, in 2001 the UN Mission in Bosnia and Herzegovina (UNMIBH) established a special trafficking operations programme to assist the local police in combating trafficking of women and girls for forced prostitution.[77]

- Offices of security institutions that are located in minority areas, and dedicated complaints mechanisms for marginalized groups. This may mean establishing presences in areas that are not necessarily the most densely populated.

- Mobile courts that provide access to justice in areas in which the judicial system is not operational. In Somaliland, for instance, mobile courts were established in 2008 in several regions of the country to facilitate access to justice for vulnerable groups living in rural and isolated areas.[78] In the eastern parts of the Democratic Republic of Congo, mobile courts with local judges, prosecutors and defence counsels were established in 2009 to try the most serious gender crimes, as well as other crimes.[79]

- Customary security and justice mechanisms that comply with fundamental human rights standards. Customary mechanisms continue to be used alongside formal security and justice mechanisms in many countries. The adaptation of the traditional *gacaca* system to hear genocide cases following the 1994 genocide in Rwanda represents one example.[80] Another is the incorporation of elements of the traditional *lisan* proceedings in the community reconciliation agreements of the Commission for Reception, Truth and Reconciliation that was established after Timor-Leste gained independence in 1999.[81] Some of the biggest challenges with many of these mechanisms are that they often do not respect basic due process standards and discriminate against women.

- Regular reporting mechanisms to assess the situation of victims and other marginalized groups. In Kosovo, for example, the Balkan Investigative Reporting Network visited courts and police stations to assess their work, investigate malpractice and produce analytical reports.[82]

Security delivery is relational: it is provided by someone for someone. In the aftermath of serious abuse, the recipients of security services need to realize that they are no longer at the mercy of violent and oppressive security institutions. Hence dealing with the past in SSR should aim not only to reform the security providers but also to empower directly victims and other marginalized groups. Empowerment efforts after conflict or authoritarian rule could include the following, among other things.

- Establishing legal aid centres and supporting civil society actors that help victims and other marginalized groups, or advocate for their rights. In Kosovo, for instance, the Center for Legal Aid and Regional Development was set up in 2007 to provide legal and social assistance and counselling to internally displaced persons, returnees, minorities and other vulnerable groups.[83] In Afghanistan, women's legal aid centres were established in 2011 to provide legal advice and counselling to women who confront domestic violence and forced marriage.[84]
- Establishing effective witness protection programmes. UNMIBH, for example, supported the establishment of a witness protection programme.[85]
- Strengthening defence counsels and supporting bar associations. For instance, both the UN Mission in Kosovo and the UN Transitional Administration in East Timor supported the development of the legal assistance sector.[86]
- Public information campaigns and targeted civil society training that make known to the public the rights and obligations they have *vis-à-vis* the security sector, and how they can enforce their rights. The campaign "Your Police Serving You" in Bosnia and Herzegovina, for instance, was an effort to increase public awareness on the principles of democratic policing.
- Strengthening the capacity of community leaders and civil society organizations to monitor security and justice actors and confront abusive behaviour. In Liberia, for example, the Liberia Media Center (LMC) was established in 2005 with international help to develop and support local media. The LMC trains journalists, assists local radio stations and serves as a watchdog for the public. In 2007 the BBC World Service Trust and the ICTJ supported the LMC in training

journalists on transitional justice reporting.[87] After the 2011 elections the LMC monitored the plans and budgets of the new government for 150 days.[88] In another example, the international NGO Avocats Sans Frontières trained 175 Timorese volunteer community leaders in law and legal procedures so they could advise rural populations on their rights.[89]

- Supporting shelters and other rehabilitation programmes for victims. In Kosovo, for instance, the International Organization for Migration supported the establishment of shelters for trafficking victims.[90]
- Supporting vocational training for victims and other marginalized groups.

Empowering victims and other marginalized groups can help them to attain full citizenship status, and allows them to know, make known and enforce their rights and needs regarding the security sector.

Strengthening accountability

If building effective accountability is fundamental to SSR in general, it is critical in the aftermath of serious abuses committed by security actors, and the reach of accountability should not only include future but also past abuses. In terms of the future, a zero-tolerance policy towards any form of further abuse should be adopted to end impunity effectively, make a clear break with the abusive past and prevent the recurrence of abuses. Multiple accountability mechanisms should be established in the security sector to do so. Accountability of the sector can be provided formally and informally. Informal accountability is provided by the activities of civil society groups such as the media, human rights organizations and other NGOs. Formal accountability mechanisms can be grouped in two categories: internal accountability, such as ethics codes, internal accountability procedures, line supervision and internal discipline; and external oversight, such as parliamentary oversight, executive oversight, independent civilian complaint and review bodies, ombudsperson services and judicial review.

In SSR in general, particular attention is often paid to establishing effective external oversight in the security sector. But experience suggests that internal discipline and external oversight functions complement each other. Internal discipline mechanisms alone run the risk of giving in to internal pressures and an inappropriate *esprit de corps* that is commonly found in security institutions, and may not enjoy the people's trust. External oversight, on the other hand, can act more independently and put pressure on the institution it monitors but cannot substitute for effective internal accountability mechanisms that have more direct access to information and can intervene more quickly and systematically. Accountability is provided more effectively, particularly in the aftermath of serious abuse, if security institutions are answerable "to multiple audiences through multiple mechanisms".[91]

In terms of the past, common approaches to SSR often prefer to ignore past abuses and only build effective accountability for any forms of future abuse. Yet in societies emerging from conflict or authoritarian rule, holding to account at least the main perpetrators of serious past abuses is an important measure to reaffirm and signal that security officials are not above the law, that impunity is not an option and that the rule of law applies universally. Accountability for serious past abuses can be provided by means of criminal prosecutions before domestic courts or possibly international tribunals and, to a certain extent, by vetting. Vetting is different from massive, summary dismissals or purges, and refers to processes for assessing an official's integrity as a means to determine his or her suitability for continued public employment. Vetting processes aim at excluding from security institutions officials who were involved in serious abuses. Doing so helps build trust by adding new faces to these institutions and reaffirming an institutional commitment to basic norms. Abusive officials are no longer protected by a culture of cronyism and exempted from accountability. Vetting also helps to dismantle abusive structures and networks that were established during the conflict or authoritarian regime and continue to be used to pursue goals related to the conflict or regime, or other crimes.[92]

Vetting provides a measure of accountability by ensuring that officers with responsibility for past abuses at least do not continue to enjoy the rewards and privileges of public office. But it is not an adequate sanction for serious abuses and should not be used as a pretext for not pursuing criminal prosecutions. Substituting a vetting process for criminal prosecutions is likely to be perceived by the victims of abuses as "cheap" justice, letting criminals off the hook.[93] But the scarcity of resources in societies emerging from conflict or authoritarian rule, as well as legal impediments and large numbers of crimes, often preclude the criminal prosecution of all abusers. Under such circumstances, vetting can help to fill the "impunity gap".[94]

However, vetting is politically sensitive and operationally complex. Political resistance to the process, operational factors such as limited institutional capacities and lack of know-how, and resource shortages and cost implications can get in the way of effective vetting. Often, a personnel census is needed to enable a vetting process because the pool of personnel needs to be determined before they can be screened. This can be done with a census and identification programme that verifies membership within one or several security institutions, identifies their institutional boundaries and helps ensure that individuals do not informally join or leave the institution(s). In so doing, a census and identification programme helps to establish the conditions for accountability after conflict. Such a programme not only provides baseline data for personnel reform, but also assists security institutions in consolidating control over their personnel, establishes the conditions to hold them accountable for their actions and introduces a measure of public accountability by making security agents identifiable to the public.[95]

Regrettably, vetting processes regularly fail because the stated objectives are overly ambitious and cannot be met within the limitations of a given context. In addition to not achieving its objective of screening out abusive officials, a failed vetting process may even contribute to legitimizing them because they can claim to have been found suitable for service. Moreover, vetting processes can be manipulated and may lead to politically motivated purges. Therefore, it is often advisable not to engage in comprehensive vetting of all personnel but to concentrate on *ad hoc* vetting of the most senior security officials, the most notorious units or the most serious perpetrators while simultaneously reinforcing the permanent accountability mechanisms that help to prevent future abuses sustainably.[96]

The de-Baathification experience in Iraq following the overthrow of the Ba'athist regime in 2003 is a case in point of how a vetting process can go wrong. The de-Baathification process dissolved the Iraqi armed forces and many of Iraq's security structures. It also dismissed from the public administration state employees in the highest levels of civil service management, as well as employees who held one of the top four levels of membership in the Ba'ath party. From its inception, de-Baathification was a deeply flawed process. The programme did not involve scrutiny of individual employees according to integrity-based criteria, and removals were not grounded on individual culpability. Rather, state employees were removed due to their association with the Ba'athist regime. The procedures were not transparent and due process standards were not respected. Lack of capacities led to uneven enforcement of de-Baathification decisions. The result was a process that was ineffective and appeared to many Iraqis to be unfair and erratic. The dissolution of the armed forces may also have contributed to the creation of the insurgency that followed, by putting hundreds of thousands of unemployed and disgruntled Iraqis on the streets.

Accountability is not incompatible with but enables the operational autonomy of security institutions, which is a condition for their fair and legal functioning. Politically driven or case-based interference in the security sector, on the other hand, undermines democratic accountability and the rule of law. Security institutions need to be shielded from arbitrary interference by political and criminal actors, the influence of primary social structures such as clans and ethnic groups should be reduced, and criminal networks that continue to misuse these institutions for personal gain or other abusive purposes have to be dismantled in order to strengthen systems of democratic accountability. In addition to vetting, measures to build the operational autonomy of security institutions include the following.

- Merit-based appointments. Ensuring that appointments and promotions are not based on political preference or affiliation but on merit can be done, for instance, by establishing merit-based appointment and promotion procedures; providing public scrutiny of appointments and promotions; and reducing the influence of executive and legislative bodies in such procedures.
- Specific procedures to ensure the operational autonomy of those holding leadership positions in security institutions. Various models exist to promote the independence of these positions. Efforts focus, in particular, on requiring professional qualifications for leadership appointments; obliging appointees to make financial and other disclosure statements; and entrusting external, independent bodies with appointment and promotion powers. The establishment of independent police commissioners in Bosnia and Herzegovina provides an example of efforts to separate policy-making from operations.[97]

- Specific measures to promote institutional loyalty. Primary social structures such as clans and ethnic groups, as well as political and unofficial armed groups, produce strong social ties between their members, particularly in environments in which other social structures have broken down or are dysfunctional. The members of primary social structures develop durable bonds among themselves and strong loyalties with the structures. These social loyalties are often in tension with the loyalties of members of the security sector to the institution they work for. Such tensions cannot be ignored. The security institution has to offer "competitive" social benefits to enhance its employees' loyalties to the institution. In addition to regular salary payments, the benefits could include social services similar to those provided by the primary social structures, such as schooling for children, medical services, pension payments, etc. A security institution could also provide pension and other payments to family members of security officials who died or were handicapped in the line of duty. Moreover, the institution could directly promote social ties among its employees by organizing social events for them; establishing dining, sports and other leisure facilities; and developing institutional signs and symbols with which the employees can associate.

A holistic approach to accountability that builds effective multiple accountability systems, makes no artificial distinctions between past and future abuses, and strengthens the operational autonomy of the security sector signals a clear break with the abusive past and a strong commitment to the democratic rule of law. A holistic approach to accountability also helps to disarticulate criminal networks within which individuals carried out and may continue to carry out criminal acts. Establishing accountability not only in the present and future but also for the past gives stronger "currency" to basic norms and values[98] and helps build trust in the security sector.

Enhancing legitimacy

Post-conflict and post-authoritarian environments pose a range of extraordinary challenges that cannot be adequately addressed with ordinary reform measures. A legacy of abuse commonly entails a fundamental crisis of trust that cannot be overcome easily. In addition to actual reform and development efforts such as those elaborated above, targeted legitimacy-building measures can help to enhance the legitimacy of security institutions and make it easier to overcome the crisis of trust.

Under normal circumstances, the people trust a security sector when it effectively and fairly provides security, and when individual cases of abuse committed by members of security agencies are sanctioned. However, in the aftermath of conflict or authoritarian rule it will be very difficult to build trust in a security sector that was involved in systematic abuses. Establishing or re-establishing its legitimacy is, therefore, a complex undertaking to convince the people, particularly those who have suffered violence and abuse, that the security sector is again, or for the first time, at their service and hence worthy of their trust.

Efforts to increase the sector's capacity and effectiveness through skills training, better equipment and improved management, efforts to provide comprehensive accountability for past, present and future abuses, efforts to promote adequate representation among the personnel of the security sector and efforts to remove undue interference from the security sector will all contribute to strengthening the legitimacy of the sector. But such reform measures may not be sufficient to restore civic trust, particularly among victims and other marginalized groups, in a security sector that was involved in systematic abuses. In addition, targeted legitimacy-building measures might be necessary to overcome this profound trust deficit and help to transform a trustworthy security sector into a trusted one. Such measures can include the following.

- Official apologies by representatives of security institutions that were involved in serious abuses. In Argentina, for instance, General Martin Balza, chief of staff of the Argentine army, read a statement on 25 April 1995 on national television acknowledging for the first time the army's involvement in systematic human rights abuses in the course of the military government that ruled the country from 1976 to 1983.[99] During this period, more than 10,000 persons were forcibly "disappeared" in Argentina. The army's establishment reacted angrily to this statement, and General Balza was excluded from the association of retired officers. Nevertheless, his example was followed in 2001 by the Peruvian joint chief of staff and in 2005 by the Chilean army's chief of staff.[100] In 2013 the Chilean association of judges issued a statement declaring that their members had failed to protect the victims of state abuse during the military regime. "The time has come to ask for forgiveness of victims … and of Chilean society," said the judges.[101]

- Memorials and museums that remember victims, acknowledge the involvement of security institutions in abuse and educate the public about past abuse. The Museum of Memory and Human Rights in Chile, for instance, is dedicated to presenting the history of the military dictatorship and documenting its abuses.[102]

- Awareness of the symbolic significance of locations in which serious abuses, such as torture or executions, occurred during the conflict. The continued use of such places by a security institution could significantly impact on its image. Such places could, on the other hand, be transformed to mark the site of a violation. For instance, Constitutional Hill in Johannesburg, South Africa, was a prison and is now South Africa's Constitutional Court.[103]

- Activities of remembrance such as commemorative days to remember victims of abuse and acknowledge the involvement of security institutions. In Argentina, the annual 24 March demonstrations mark the beginning of the 1970s' military dictatorship. In Peru, relatives of the disappeared joined efforts to knit a gigantic "scarf of hope" in memory of victims.

- The renaming of streets and public places that bear the names of security officials or institutions with histories of abuse.

- The removal or replacement of monuments that relate to security officials or institutions with histories of abuse. In Vienna, Austria, a secret homage to the Nazi regime was discovered in 2012 in a sculpture that honours soldiers killed during the Second World War. Subsequently, the minister of defence decided to redesign the entire memorial site, but met resistance from right-wing politicians. Plans to establish a monument for army deserters during the Nazi period continued to spark controversies.[104]

- The changing of the oath of office to ensure that it refers to fundamental norms and values, and providing public access to the ceremony in which security officials take the oath of office.

- The changing of coats of arms, insignia and uniforms that are associated with an abusive past. In post-conflict contexts, getting the

   Alexander Mayer-Rieckh

police to wear blue uniforms rather than green military uniforms often represents a significant symbolic change. The struggle over insignia in Bosnia and Herzegovina provides another example of the importance of changing symbols.

- Institution-based truth-seeking efforts. An institution that is being re-established or reformed has to take into account its abusive past, come to terms with it and mark a new beginning that distances it from the legacy of abuse. New recruits as well as longstanding officials have to know about the abusive past in order to dissociate themselves from it and build a common culture of "never again". The security institution could make use of its institutional spaces and life-cycle events, such as its graduation ceremonies, anniversary or open days, to help its personnel to remember and renounce the abusive past and construct a new institutional identity.

Such targeted legitimacy-building measures verbally or symbolically reaffirm a commitment to overcome the legacy of abuse and an endorsement of democratic norms and values. Unlike measures to increase a security sector's effectiveness or enhance accountability and representation in the sector, these measures do not "promote trust through action", but they do so by acknowledging past abuses, clearly "signalling" a turning away from an abusive past and reaffirming a commitment to the democratic rule of law.[105] Obviously, such signalling measures can only complement but not replace actual structural reforms. Stand-alone verbal or symbolic reaffirmations of norms that are not accompanied by actions to give effect to these norms are "empty words" that lack credibility. Nevertheless, signals can be important complements to actions when the seriousness of past abuse makes it hard to convince the people of the sector's trustworthiness. Such signals may help to persuade the people that the actual reform efforts are not superficial but represent a true change of heart. As a result, these signals may help doubtful people begin – again or for the first time – trusting a trustworthy security sector.

It is needless to say that such signalling measures can easily be abused for the purposes of partisan political battles in the present. For instance, the establishment of the House of Terror in Budapest, which chronicles the darkest aspects of Hungary's past,[106] has been criticized for equating communism with fascism and for intending to tarnish the image of the socialist party and its communist past.[107] The choice of topics and their categorization in the context of signalling measures are often controversial, particularly when the past is contested. They can promote trust only when they are performed by a representative of an institution that was responsible for the abuses, relate to established abuses, acknowledge them as abuses, signal a turning away from them and are not a substitute for other transitional justice efforts.

Framework of case study analysis

The following sections examine two countries in transition that were confronted with legacies of massive abuse. Bosnia and Herzegovina after the 1995 Dayton Peace Agreement had to face not only the consequences of a vicious three-and-a-half-year armed conflict but also the legacy of communism. Nepal embarked on a peace process following the 2006 Comprehensive Peace Agreement that brought a formal end to the brutal ten-year armed conflict between government forces and Maoist insurgents. Each of the two case studies is divided into three subsections. The first provides a brief overview of the conflict and the subsequent peace agreement, focusing on the role of the security sector. The second contains an analysis of the security sector after the conflict and the SSR process. Particular attention is paid to the effects of the abusive history, and specifically whether it has led to exclusion, impunity and distrust. The concluding subsection of each case study seeks to identify steps that have been taken to deal with the abusive past, particularly in terms of strengthening accountability, promoting inclusion and enhancing legitimacy, and see how these steps – or the lack thereof – have affected the SSR process. Rather than comprehensively discussing each of the steps, the focus is on those that help us to understand in what ways dealing with the past affects SSR.

POLICE REFORM IN BOSNIA AND HERZEGOVINA BETWEEN 1995 AND 2002[108]

The conflict and the Dayton Peace Agreement

In communist Yugoslavia, the country's six republics had their own law enforcement systems and each police force formed an integral part of the republic's ministry of interior. A minister who was a member of the communist hierarchy and managed all operational and personnel aspects of the police headed the ministry. The government was dominated by the Communist Party, and party membership was a condition for professional advancement of public officials, including police officers. When nationalist parties came to power in Yugoslavia following the breakdown of communism and the 1990 elections, they took control of the state apparatus, including the police.

Bosnia and Herzegovina, one of Yugoslavia's six republics, was located in the middle of the country surrounded by Croatia, Serbia and Montenegro. In contrast to Slovenia and Croatia, no national group had an absolute majority in pre-conflict Bosnia and Herzegovina. According to the 1991 census, the republic had a population of 4.4 million inhabitants, of whom 43.7 per cent declared themselves Bosniak,[109] 31 per cent Serb, 17.3 per cent Croat and 7.6 per cent Yugoslav or another nationality.[110]

Following Bosnia and Herzegovina's declaration of independence from Yugoslavia in February 1992, conflict quickly erupted among its Bosniaks, Serbs and Croats, and the country plunged into all-out war.[111] Both Bosnian Serbs and Bosnian Croats were actively supported by regular Serbian and Croatian forces, i.e. the Yugoslav National Army (JNA) and the Croatian

Defence Force (HVO), and sought to split off large parts of the territory of Bosnia and Herzegovina. Bosnian government (Bosniak) forces fought to preserve a unitary state that would maintain the borders of the Republic of Bosnia and Herzegovina in the former Yugoslavia. Assault on civilian populations, especially the forced migration of people on the basis of their ethnicity (what became infamously known as "ethnic cleansing"), was not only an instrument of warfare but above all a central aspect of the political project the war was intended to accomplish. In particular, Bosnian Serb and Bosnian Croat forces dispossessed, displaced, interned, ill treated, raped and killed populations to enlarge the territory they controlled. During the atrocious three-and-a-half-year armed conflict more than 100,000 people were killed[112] and an estimated 2.2 million (around half the population) were displaced.[113]

After the outbreak of the conflict, Bosnian Serb and Bosnian Croat leaders seized the public institutions in their "autonomous areas", including the police.[114] The police now served nationalist enclaves and turned into an instrument of war, participating in the execution of "ethnic cleansing". The transition from law enforcement to war-fighting was all the easier because the police in communist Yugoslavia had a paramilitary role in the national defence system, in addition to regular law enforcement and state security roles. In times of war, the police were to support territorial defence in the interior of the country. During the conflict the military and police conducted joint operations, and soldiers and members of paramilitary groups without formal police training joined the police.

International efforts to resolve the conflict were intense, but indecisive and ineffective. This only changed conclusively due to public outrage following the fall of the UN-designated safe areas of Srebrenica and Zepa in July 1995 and the international community's new resolve to use force.[115] Following the agreement of the Bosnian Croats and Bosniaks to ally themselves in the Federation of Bosnia and Herzegovina,[116] Croat and Bosniak forces launched successful offences against the Serbian forces, which at last set the necessary conditions for a settlement.

The three-and-a-half-year conflict ended with the General Framework Agreement for Peace in Bosnia and Herzegovina, the so-called Dayton Peace Agreement, which was negotiated in November 1995 under strong US pressure at the air force base in Dayton, Ohio, and signed in Paris on 14 December 1995.[117] The agreement had essentially two objectives: to end the fighting, and to build a viable, democratic state of Bosnia and Herzegovina. While the parties carried primary responsibility to implement the agreement, it designated a broad array of international organizations to assist the process, including the Office of the High Representative; the multinational Implementation Force (IFOR), which was succeeded by the Stabilization Force (SFOR) after one year; the Organization for Security and Cooperation in Europe (OSCE); the UN Mission in Bosnia and Herzegovina with its International Police Task Force (IPTF); and the UN High Commissioner for Refugees. The Dayton Peace Agreement was a "coerced compromise" rather than a sincere agreement, and yet it relied primarily on those responsible for the war to implement the peace.[118] Nationalist Bosnian Serbs and Bosnian Croats fiercely resisted the implementation of the agreement, as its objectives were contrary to the very reasons why they began the war and implementing it would have reversed the war's outcomes. Significantly, they were not committed to the two fundamental provisions of the peace agreement: the territorial integrity of Bosnia and Herzegovina in its pre-conflict borders, and the right to return of all displaced persons. While Dayton ended the fighting, the conflict continued by other means. This left a heavy responsibility on the international implementers, who were ill equipped to fulfil it.

The constitution of the Dayton Peace Agreement provided for weak state structures.[119] Bosnia and Herzegovina would consist of two coequal "entities", the Federation of Bosnia and Herzegovina and the Republika Srpska, and all governmental functions except the few expressly assigned to the state would fall under the responsibilities of these entities. In the Federation of Bosnia and Herzegovina authority was further devolved to ten cantons in order to create a delicate balance of power between Bosniaks and Bosnian Croats.[120] Regular policing functions fell under the mandate of the two entities.[121] In the federation, the ten cantons had primary responsibility for police.[122] As a result, the post-Dayton policing systems were highly fragmented and remained vulnerable to interference by local leaders with nationalist agendas. There were 12 ministries of interior, each with its own police service: the Republika Srpska Ministry of Interior, the Federation Ministry of Interior and ten cantonal ministries of interior. Brčko district had its own police department in accordance with its special status. This compares with one ministry of interior for the entire territory of pre-conflict Bosnia and Herzegovina.

Map 1: Bosnia and Herzegovina after the Dayton Peace Agreement

The police after Dayton

In terms of police reform, the parties committed themselves in the Dayton Peace Agreement to "provide a safe and secure environment for all persons in their respective jurisdictions, by maintaining civilian law enforcement agencies operating in accordance with internationally recognized standards and with respect for internationally recognized human rights and fundamental freedoms",[123] and to ensure the "prosecution, dismissal or transfer, as appropriate" of police officers responsible for serious abuses of the basic rights of minorities.[124]

The Dayton Peace Agreement designated the IPTF to assist in the reform of the police and entrusted the United Nations to run it.[125] The Security Council established UNMIBH, which included the IPTF under the responsibility of a UN civilian office.[126] Initially, the IPTF included 1,721 international police officers, a number later increased to 2,027.[127] In addition, UNMIBH included 254 international civilian staff and 811 local personnel. The IPTF was slow to deploy, short of logistical support and only reached its full strength in late 1996.[128] UNMIBH did not have an executive mandate and had only limited enforcement powers *vis-à-vis* the parties. It was to monitor, advise and train local police officers, and to assist and facilitate the reform process.[129] Reforming the police would require the consent and support of the domestic authorities. In 1996 the UN Security Council strengthened the mandate of UNMIBH, providing it with the power to conduct independent investigations into abuses by the local police.[130]

The reasons for deciding to reform the existing police rather than to establish a new force were largely political. The international community was not willing to commit the resources that establishing a new police would have required, particularly the need to deploy an international interim police force. Nevertheless, some have argued that Dayton should have mandated the IPTF with creating a new police rather than with reforming the existing forces.[131] Arguably, this might have made for an easier transition to the democratic rule of law. At the same time, disbanding entire security institutions is not without risks. In particular, demobilized officers can create serious security problems. Moreover, disbanding the police can result in serious law enforcement gaps that are difficult to fill by international police forces. Finally, the establishment of a new police would not have been a short-cut to avoid the challenges of dealing with the abusive past.

By the end of the conflict the number of active police officers in Bosnia and Herzegovina had reportedly swelled to an estimated 44,750, a threefold increase of their pre-war size.[132] This meant that, with a total population of approximately 4 million,[133] there were 1,119 police officers per 100,000 inhabitants in Bosnia and Herzegovina. These figures exceeded by far generally accepted practice – a UN survey indicates a median of approximately 300 police officers per 100,000 inhabitants worldwide.[134] In

Europe the number of police officers is frequently even lower: there are 406 police officers per 100,000 inhabitants in Italy, 301 officers in Germany and 384 in France, but the Netherlands has 215, Denmark has 195 and Norway has only 155 police officers per 100,000 inhabitants.[135]

Rather than upholding the rule of law and human rights, the post-Dayton police continued to support nationalist separatist agendas and function in separate nationality-based forces, each operating under the direct control of the respective nationalist political party. There was no police cooperation between the two entities, and the Bosnian Croat police operated autonomously within the federation. Freedom of movement was blocked by police checkpoints along the inter-entity boundary line and between Bosniak and Bosnian Croat communities in the federation. Particularly in Bosnian Croat and Bosnian Serb areas, minority returnees were not protected during home visits, and minority-related incidents were not investigated. The police forces themselves had war criminals among their ranks. For instance, the International Crisis Group identified in 2000 in the Republika Srpska 75 officials and other individuals who were alleged to have participated in war crimes. Of these, 20 were police officers and Ministry of Interior officials, including a chief of police, two advisers to the minister, a director of customs and a head of a criminal department.[136] As a result, the police continued to discriminate against, harass and intimidate minority populations. The absence of functional law enforcement created a climate of impunity, subverting a fundamental clause of the Dayton Peace Agreement: the promise that all refugees and displaced persons could voluntarily and safely return.

During the initial months after its establishment, the IPTF not only struggled operationally but also received little cooperation from the various domestic police forces and ministries of interior. Matters seemed to improve when UNMIBH convened, in April 1996, a conference on police restructuring in Petersberg near Bonn in Germany, which was attended by officials from the Federation of Bosnia and Herzegovina, UN officials and donor-country representatives. Republika Srpska officials were also invited but refused to attend. The population were not consulted prior to the conference, and civil society representatives were not invited.

The so-called Bonn-Petersberg Agreement was signed on 25 April 1996 and provided, among other things, for a reduction of the police forces to levels consistent with European standards; a mixed composition of the police that would reflect the last pre-war population census of 1991; new uniforms with federation insignia that would be used by all federation police officers; a commitment to accepted international policing principles as articulated by the conference; the development and implementation of training standards and curricula by the IPTF; and the screening and certification of police officers by the IPTF. The restructuring of the police was to proceed on a phased basis, canton by canton, and to be completed no later than September 1996.[137]

This schedule would have been unrealistic under the most conducive circumstances. In post-conflict Bosnia and Herzegovina, signing but not implementing agreements became almost a strategy of the former warring factions to undermine the peace agreement and continue the pursuit of conflict-related goals. While some progress was made over the next years in Bosniak-dominated cantons, and the police academy in Sarajevo was reopened in December 1997 with a first mixed class of Bosniak and Bosnian Croat cadets, reform and restructuring of the police were fiercely resisted in the Bosnian Croat-dominated cantons and made little headway in the mixed cantons. The Republika Srpska did not even sign a police restructuring agreement until December 1998.

Policing in the municipality of Stolac in the federation's Herzegovina-Neretva canton was a case in point.[138] Following the conflict, Herzegovina-Neretva was a mixed Bosnian Croat-Bosniak canton. The population was segregated in Bosniak and Bosnian Croat municipalities, and the municipal administrations were either Bosnian Croat or Bosniak. Houses and apartments of refugees and displaced persons were illegally occupied by majority populations, and minority returns did not take place in the immediate post-conflict period. The cantonal administration was not integrated. The Bosniak and Bosnian Croat administrations operated separately. The two nationalities used different currencies, different flags and insignia, different numberplates, different school systems and different mobile phone networks. Mostar, the cantonal capital, was a divided city. East Mostar was Bosniak administered, West Mostar was Bosnian Croat administered. The old bridge over the River Neretva, the symbol of Mostar that linked the two parts of city and had been destroyed during the conflict, was not restored and the Neretva was a boundary not crossed.

In accordance with the Bonn-Petersberg Agreement, cantonal police were formed in Herzegovina-Neretva in 1997. However, the police were never integrated and continued to operate in two separate forces in parallel chains of command from different buildings. Surplus officers were not demobilized and Bosnian Serb officers were initially not recruited.

Stolac is located not far from Mostar in southeastern Herzegovina. Before the armed conflict it had a population of more than 18,000 inhabitants, of whom 44 per cent were Bosniak, 33 per cent Bosnian Croat and 21 per cent Bosnian Serb. During the conflict most Bosnian Serbs and Bosniaks had to leave Stolac, and the majority of their houses were destroyed by Bosnian Croat military and paramilitary forces. The post-conflict population of Stolac was estimated at 8,000 Bosnian Croat inhabitants, including 3,000–4,000 internally displaced people. The public administration was taken over by Bosnian Croats. From 1993 through most of 1997, all police were Bosnian Croat in Stolac. Following the inauguration of the cantonal police, the first Bosniak police officers were assigned to the Stolac police but did not live in the municipality.

In early 1998 agreements were reached on phased minority returns to most municipalities in the Herzegovina-Neretva canton, including Stolac. Policing was ineffective in Stolac when it came to minority returns, organized crime and war criminals. When the security situation deteriorated in minority return areas throughout 1998, the police did not take adequate measures in crime prevention and detection. During the return season of 1998 UNMIBH registered over 70 incidents of returnee-related violence in Stolac. These included explosions, fires, beatings and intimidations. In the neighbouring municipality of Capljina, a recently arrived Bosniak returnee was killed when a grenade was thrown at his house on 2 October 1998. The response of the police was ineffective and unprofessional. Security plans lacked precision and were not adhered to. Patrols to areas of recent incidents were not increased or did not occur at all. Investigations were carried out superficially and produced no significant results. During 1998 not one suspect was prosecuted in relation to the more than 70 returnee-related incidents in Stolac. Continually, the police failed to live up to their commitments, which had been made in the Dayton Peace Agreement and numerous subsequent agreements and declarations. The absence of effective policing created a climate of impunity in which further incidents directed against minority returnees were tolerated or even encouraged.

An illegal market near Stolac at the inter-entity boundary line with the Republika Srpska, the so-called Renner Market, was allowed to operate despite clear evidence of trade in stolen goods such as cars embezzled in Germany, and smuggling of cigarettes and other merchandise. The market was run by the Renner Transport Company, which was reportedly involved in transnational criminal activity, including human trafficking, and in organizing violent resistance against Bosniak minority returns to Stolac. In January 1999 its owner, Jozo Peric, was arrested by the cantonal police with active SFOR support. The investigating judge released him in March 1999, however, due to lack of evidence. According to the IPTF, the local police investigations had been slow, passive and disinterested. Additional evidence could have been uncovered if the local police had followed the advice of IPTF officers.[139]

Stolac police also failed to take effective action against war crimes suspects. This was particularly evident in separate incidents in 2000 and 2001 when the police came in direct contact with indicted war criminals but failed to arrest them. In one incident, the chief of the uniformed police had been hand-delivered the arrest warrant by the Bosniak cantonal deputy interior minister. Furthermore, many Bosnian Croat police officers pledged 3 per cent of their salaries to the families of Croats awaiting trial in The Hague when asked to do so by the cantonal prime minister.

These operational shortcomings point, among other things, to a failure to break with the conflict past. While military battles and violent ethnic cleansing had been effectively stopped by the international military intervention and the international presence established after Dayton, the conflict continued by any means tolerated by the international community. The goals of the conflict also continued to determine the practices of policing throughout many parts of Bosnia and Herzegovina. In Stolac this was evident in inappropriate external interference in the police by nationalist political parties and criminal groups, which frequently interacted with police officers; a failure to integrate the Bosniak minority police officers, who used separate offices, followed a separate chain of command, were paid differently, jointly left the municipality at night because they did not feel safe and whose families did not move to Stolac for security reasons; the presence of former Bosnian Croat soldiers in the police, who had not received any police training and some of whom were reportedly involved in war crimes; the refusal to take action against war criminals; and the failure to demobilize surplus Bosnian Croat police officers despite statements of cantonal officials to have done so in accordance with the Bonn-Petersberg Agreement. Also the "signals" sent by the police in Stolac revealed an unwillingness to break with the conflict past. As in other Bosnian Croat majority areas, the Stolac police not only failed to display federation and state insignia but also continued to use Croat flags, badges and other symbols related to the illegal "Croat Republic of Herceg Bosna". During an inspection of the Stolac police station in late 1998, UNMIBH found on display in offices pictures of the Croatian President Franjo Tudjman, the late Croatian Defence Minister Gojko Susak, who hailed originally from Herzegovina, the Croatian King Tomislav, the Ustasha leader Ante Pavelic and a map of "Greater Croatia" that included the entire territory of Bosnia and Herzegovina.[140] Bosnian Croat officers frequently visited a coffee bar in front of the police station which displayed above its entrance a large Ustasha flag.

Despite written agreements and oral commitments to address some aspects of the police's conflict legacy, reform efforts in the immediate post-Dayton period focused more on "training and equipping" the police forces of the country, underestimated the perseverance of nationalist groups in the pursuit of conflict goals and were ineffective in addressing the effects of the conflict. Without doing so, police reform could not succeed in building services that operate "in accordance with internationally recognized standards and with respect for internationally recognized human rights and fundamental freedoms", as stipulated by the Dayton Peace Agreement.[141]

Dealing with the past of the police in Bosnia and Herzegovina

Gradually, the international community grew more and more impatient with the intransigence of the dominant nationalist groups and became more assertive in its efforts to realize the Dayton Agreement. In this context, UNMIBH also adopted a more robust approach in response to nationalist resistance against police reform. On the basis of the Bonn-Petersberg Agreement, UN Security Council Resolution 1088 and the December 1998 police restructuring agreement with the other entity of Bosnia and Herzegovina, the Republika Srpska,[142] UNMIBH developed the power to decertify police officers. From 1999 onwards the conflict legacy was addressed more directly and proactively in police reform, and various measures were initiated to promote the inclusion of all people, strengthen the accountability of the police and enhance their legitimacy.

To promote the *inclusion* of minorities, reinforced efforts were made to increase their recruitment into the police, which was also to facilitate the return of displaced persons.[143] The programme involved identifying potential minority candidates, reserving places for minority cadets in the police academies, retraining police officers who had left the service during the armed conflict, supporting voluntary redeployments of minority officers and helping them to identify housing for their families, publicity campaigns advertising the recruitment of minority police officers and recruitment campaigns to encourage female enrolment at the academies.[144] As a result, there was an average of around 10 per cent minority officers and around 3 per cent female officers in December 2002.[145]

In mixed Bosniak-Bosnian Croat cantons, concerted efforts were made to remove the parallel chains of command in the ministries of interior and fully integrate the structures of the police by establishing joint office locations, eliminating duplicate positions, integrating the budgets of the ministries of interior and fully integrating the chain of command.[146] Moreover, UNMIBH with domestic police services launched a campaign called "Your Police Serving You" to increase public awareness of the principles of democratic policing.[147] The police also organized community open days, school visits and public demonstrations of policing skills. The population were not consulted on police reform, however, and civil society has not been given an opportunity to participate in the reform process.

To strengthen the *accountability* of the police, all officers were registered to ensure the agreed reduction of numbers, determine the composition of the police forces and establish the conditions for holding officers to account for their actions, including crimes committed during the conflict.[148] Uniform ID cards were issued to all police officers making them identifiable to the public. Officers were also screened and vetted on, among other things, criminal records, educational records, professional performance, war crimes records, illegal housing and corruption.[149] Information on the background of police officers was drawn from, among other sources, databases of the International Criminal Tribunal of the former Yugoslavia. The types of cases reviewed included police officers who were guards or interrogators in concentration camps and took part in ill treatment of prisoners; commanders of military units that operated detention facilities where atrocities occurred; and officers who were directly involved in war crimes or crimes against humanity, including murder, rape and torture. As a result of the vetting process, 481 police officers out of the total of 15,786 throughout Bosnia and Herzegovina were removed from the police, while the cases of 228 officers were pending in December 2002.[150]

The property status of more than 8,300 police officers whose pre-conflict addresses differed from their current addresses was also checked. Illegal occupants had to regularize their housing situation or would be removed from the police. Of the 7,998 illegal occupant officers, around 80 per cent vacated the property they occupied and 20 per cent entered into rental agreements with the rightful owners.[151]

Independent police commissioners were established in all cantons of the federation and the two entities to reduce political interference in police work and build the operational autonomy of the police. Police commissioners had to be career police officers and wear uniform while on duty. They were appointed by independent boards with civil society representatives. While a police commissioner was to be politically accountable to the respective minister of interior, the commissioner was to be solely responsible for the management and operations of the police.[152]

Some efforts were also made to enhance the legitimacy of the police and increase public trust. Among other things, uniform vehicle licence plates were introduced throughout the country in 1998, significantly improving freedom of movement. In July 1999 the high representative issued a decision prohibiting the use of non-neutral or offensive insignia by the police and judicial institutions in the federation.[153] As a result, many but not all nationalist insignia were removed from these institutions.[154] Generally, the nationalist elites in power remained unapologetic about the past.

This reinvigorated approach to police reform yielded certain results. Unqualified or unsuitable officers were removed, the overall number of officers was verified and reduced, the ethnic composition of the forces was improved and the number of female officers was increased. The reform efforts also positively affected the performance of the police in minority return areas, and possibly the return process itself. In Stolac the number of attacks and other violent incidents targeting minority returnees decreased following the removal of police officers with bad human rights track records and the further inclusion of minority officers in the Stolac police administration in 1999.[155] According to a public opinion survey commissioned by the UN Development Programme (UNDP), overall public confidence in the police rose during the period the police services were restructured with the assistance of UNMIBH.[156] Minority returnees generally expressed greater trust in the police following the integration of minority officers and the removal of human rights abusers.[157] In 2002 the International Crisis Group judged that after "three years of intensified reform efforts, Bosnia's police forces have begun to justify the decision taken at Dayton that they should be reformed rather than replaced".[158]

Unsurprisingly, resistance by nationalist groups to the reforms increased rather than decreased between 1999 and 2002, since addressing the conflict legacy within the police directly attacked some of the root causes of the conflict and threatened the broader gains these groups had made during the fighting. Reforming the police also meant that nationalist groups would lose an effective instrument to pursue their goals with non-military means. Social conflicts play themselves out within the structures of the police but cannot be resolved by internal reforms alone. Police reform is constrained by the existing "political geography" of a given society, and depends on broader political and social processes to succeed.[159] Hence effectively continuing the police reform would have meant working proactively within the police in the context of an overall political reform process.

Did the interventionist approach pursued by the international community during this period undermine the principle of local ownership that is so fundamental in SSR? This was a controversial question in Bosnia and Herzegovina after Dayton, and stirred much debate both among domestic constituencies and in the international community.[160] Who is to own? Can local ownership be allowed to undermine the existence of the state itself? To what extent and for how long are international transitional interventions legitimate and acceptable? These important questions cannot be adequately explored in the context of this paper. Obviously, reform processes in the absence of commitment and ownership on the part of those undertaking them are not sustainable and will not succeed.[161] In fact, controversy over the vetting process continued long after UNMIBH had left.[162] But the constituencies committed to the democratic rule of law and willing to own an SSR process were weak and marginalized in Bosnia and Herzegovina. Rather than gradually turning the country into a protectorate and paralysing domestic processes for many years after Dayton, international efforts should have focused early and decisively on disempowering those who continued to pursue the goals of the conflict and empowering reform-minded constituencies that could have carried forward the reform process.

Rather than allowing discredited security actors and nationalist politicians to own the SSR process, the early and proactive participation of marginalized groups which supported the Dayton project might have helped to move the SSR process forward.

The police reform process was far from complete when UNMIBH came to an end in 2002, and much remained to be done to establish effective, accountable and affordable police services in Bosnia and Herzegovina. Unfortunately, this did not happen to the extent necessary. In 2002 UNMIBH was replaced by the European Police Mission (EUPM), which had a mandate only to monitor, mentor and inspect. The EUPM interpreted its mandate narrowly and approached police reform as a technical, operational and merely forward-looking task that insufficiently acknowledged the political, administrative and social dimensions of reforming a police after conflict, including the challenge of addressing the conflict's legacy.[163] Police reform after 2002 is beyond the scope of this case study.[164]

REFORMING THE SECURITY SECTOR IN NEPAL[165]

The conflict and the Comprehensive Peace Agreement

Nepal is bordered to the north by China and to the south, east and west by India. It has a population of approximately 27 million, with a great diversity of ethnic groups and castes.[166] Throughout most of its history Nepal was a monarchy. In 1990 several political parties in Nepal formed a broad alliance and launched the so-called People's Movement (Jana Andolan), which led to a period of turbulent street protests. The Jana Andolan brought about the end of absolute monarchy, and a constitutional monarchy with a multi-party parliament was established in May 1991. But popular expectations of social progress and greater equality remained largely unfulfilled in the years to come. Particularly members of the lowest Hindu caste, the Dalits, and non-Hindu ethnic groups, the Janajatis, continued to be excluded from economic opportunities and political empowerment.[167] In 1996 the newly formed Communist Party of Nepal (Maoist) (CPN-M) and its armed wing, the People's Liberation Army (PLA), launched an armed struggle, the so-called People's War, against the state. From 1996 to 2006 Nepal experienced a brutal armed conflict between government forces and Maoist insurgents.

During the first years of the conflict the Nepal Police was predominantly tasked with fighting the PLA. But the police were unable to quell the insurgency and the majority of police posts throughout the country ceased to function.[168] In 2001 the government declared a state of emergency, deployed the Royal Nepal Army (now the Nepal Army) and put in place a paramilitary force, the Armed Police Force (APF), to mount large-scale counterinsurgency operations. Security personnel were vested with wide powers of warrantless arrest and detention without charge to counter what were termed "terrorist activities". As a result, the army doubled its strength from around 45,000 to more than 90,000 personnel.[169] From the time it was deployed, the army had *de facto* control over the police and the APF, even though a formal unified command structure under the military was established only in 2003. According to estimates, there were between 5,000 and 10,000 active PLA combatants for much of the conflict period.[170] In the following years the military confrontation intensified significantly, the number of killings increased drastically and the number of abuses committed by all parties – particularly by the army, the police and the APF, but also by the PLA – rose sharply. Neither side respected international humanitarian and human rights law, and thousands of civilians including women and children were executed, tortured, raped, made to disappear or arbitrarily arrested and detained. The conflict left at least 13,000 people dead and over 1,300 missing.[171] According to reports received by the Office of the UN High Commissioner for Human Rights (OHCHR), up to 9,000 serious human rights or humanitarian law violations have been committed during the decade-long conflict, including over 2,000 unlawful killings, around 1,000 enforced disappearances and more than 2,500 cases of torture or serious ill treatment. In addition, the OHCHR recorded numerous cases of sexual violence and arbitrary arrest.[172]

The second Jana Andolan in 2005–2006, the 12-point agreement of November 2005 and the 2006 Comprehensive Peace Agreement (CPA) brought an end to the armed conflict and put Nepal on the road to building a democratic state based on the rule of law. At the request of the government and the CPN-M, the UN Security Council established in 2007 the UN Mission in Nepal (UNMIN) to assist and help build confidence in the peace process, including through its arms-monitoring responsibilities. The interim constitution came into force in January 2007, and in April 2008 the Constituent Assembly was elected and the monarchy was abolished.

The CPA, the interim constitution and several subsequent agreements include five aspects that have been unchanging and are fundamental to the peace process: a commitment to power sharing and consensus between the major parliamentary parties and the Maoists; a commitment by the Maoists

Map 2:   Nepal

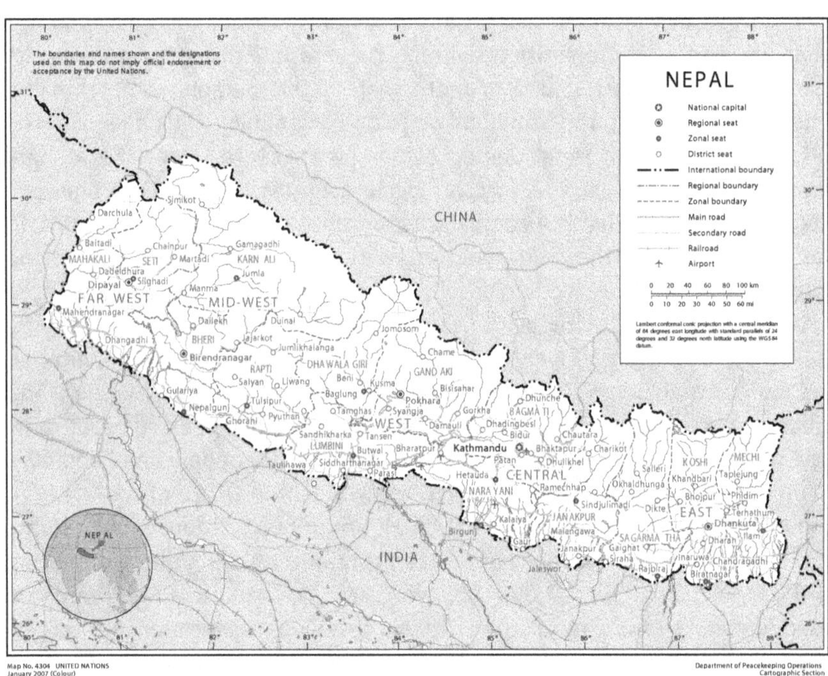

Map No. 4304 UNITED NATIONS
January 2007 (Colour)
Department of Peacekeeping Operations
Cartographic Section

to the transformation of their movement, and to respect the rule of law and democratic processes; a commitment to reforming the security sector; a commitment to political, economic and social reform and development; and a commitment to address the needs of victims of the conflict and build the rule of law by ending impunity.

Army, police and former combatants after the conflict

The commitment to reform the security sector focused on the "integration and rehabilitation" of former Maoist combatants and the "democratization" of the army, including, among other things, determining its appropriate size, democratic restructuring and providing human rights training.[173] The CPA, the interim constitution and subsequent agreements said little about other aspects of SSR and initially did not envisage comprehensive reform covering the need to develop a national security policy, the reform of other security actors such as the APF, the Maoist militia or the intelligence service, and the need to develop strong civil oversight and democratic control of the security sector. Being more explicit about these aspects in the agreements and adopting a more holistic approach to SSR would have been desirable. At the same time, the transformation of the army and the role of the former Maoist combatants in the army were the most critical SSR questions and were at the core of Nepal's peace process.[174] Moreover, a broader debate on SSR started in the Constituent Assembly in the context of the constitution drafting process.[175]

Progress in the peace process has been uneven and a number of commitments made in the CPA, interim constitution and other agreements have not been honoured, including the pledges to reform the security sector. On 1 November 2011 the parties finally reached an agreement on the integration and rehabilitation of the Maoist combatants, as well as on the process to complete the writing of the constitution.[176] But the issue of democratizing the army remained absent from the November 2011 agreement.

Throughout 2012 former Maoist combatants were screened for integration into the army. The US State Department removed the Maoists from its list of terrorist organizations in September 2012. The integration of 1,460 former Maoist combatants was completed in August 2013. Moreover, the cross-party Special Committee for Supervision, Integration and Rehabilitation of Maoist Combatants recommended the government to establish a 4,171-strong non-combat general directorate for former combatants.

But the army continued to resist any plans for its democratization and largely enjoyed independence from politicians. While the overall legislative structure for democratic oversight of the army was in place, there has not been the political will to make it a reality.[177] The Ministry of Defence remained weak and the National Security Council did not function effectively. The army largely failed to cooperate with the civilian justice system and parliamentary committees did not pursue difficult questions of transparency, oversight and reform of the military.[178] At the same time, the police remained under the control of the government. The government had the power to issue directives to the police and could dismiss higher-ranking officers. As a result, the police lacked operational autonomy in carrying out their tasks. Moreover, there was no independent oversight body to which the public could complain about police misconduct.[179]

The peace process in Nepal is cited as an example of ownership of the process by the former warring factions, and has seen progress in certain areas.[180] However, with the exception of the integration and rehabilitation of former Maoist combatants, the SSR process did not move forward significantly during the first six years after the armed conflict came to an end. Particularly the army only paid lip service to the commitments made in the CPA, the interim constitution and other agreements, and did not accept the framework of democracy and the rule of law.

Not dealing with the past of the Nepalese security sector

The parties to the CPA, the interim constitution and other relevant agreements committed to address the needs of victims of the conflict and build the rule of law by ending impunity.[181] Concretely, they vowed to investigate the fate of the disappeared, repair victims of the conflict, establish a truth commission and take action against those responsible for serious human rights violations. The 12-point agreement of 2005 states that, regarding cases of inappropriate conduct in the past, "a common commitment has been expressed to investigate the incidents ... and to take action over the guilty".[182] The 2006 CPA stated that the truth and reconciliation commission would have the responsibility to find out "the truth about those who committed the gross violations of human rights and were involved in crimes against humanity in the course of the conflict".[183] The 2007 interim constitution guaranteed the right to remedy for those whose fundamental rights have been violated.[184]

These written obligations have been reaffirmed in repeated statements by various officials. On several occasions the government stated its intention to end impunity. For instance, it issued a statement during the conflict period that included, among other things, a promise to "hold accountable those responsible for any such [human rights] violations".[185] In their Constituent Assembly election manifestos in 2008, the major political parties pledged to end impunity.[186] On 26 September 2008 then Prime Minister Pushpa Kamal Dahal "Prachanda" told the UN General Assembly that the government was committed to ending impunity. Also the Nepal Army, the Nepal Police and the APF repeatedly made public statements on accountability and have issued rules and procedures to sanction human rights violations.[187]

Nepal's domestic law penalizes most offences that amount to serious violations of human rights or international humanitarian law, and includes procedures to investigate and prosecute such offences. The army and the police also operate several internal accountability mechanisms, including discipline regimes and human rights sections.

Little has been accomplished in practice, however, to establish *accountability* for past abuses. Despite the multiple layers of accountability mechanisms in place, not one person in Nepal has been prosecuted in a civilian court for serious human rights or humanitarian law violations committed during the conflict. The police have failed to investigate such violations due to political interference, lack of oversight, fear of the army and implication in abuses by the police force itself. The army has stated that it has conducted military proceedings against its members for such violations, but has not substantiated these claims.[188]

Not only has the army failed to suspend or remove officers accused of involvement in serious human rights abuses, but it has promoted them to senior ranks.[189] As late as November 2012 the Supreme Court asked the government to explain its decision to promote a colonel to brigadier-general after allegations of his involvement in torture and forced disappearances of Maoist combatants during the conflict.[190] The police have also promoted rather than investigated officers alleged to have committed serious crimes during the conflict.[191] Moreover, the judiciary failed to stop such promotions. For instance, following the promotion of a police officer who was a suspect in a disappearance case, the Supreme Court held in 2011 that a recommendation by the National Human Rights Commission to prosecute the suspect did not represent a sufficient basis to suspend his promotion pending the outcome of the investigations.[192]

This pervasive culture of impunity in Nepal expressed itself not only in the successful obstruction of criminal prosecutions but also in the failure to establish a vetting mechanism to screen out security officers who had committed serious violations of human rights or humanitarian law.[193] Moreover, the government and lawmakers have proposed empowering the future truth and reconciliation commission to grant amnesties for international crimes and gross violations of international law committed during the conflict, in contravention to international law.[194] According to one political leader in December 2011, the political parties have "agreed to go for reconciliation and amnesty instead of prosecution for all kinds of crimes because this is what we believe is key to securing lasting peace".[195]

The fact that the army has sent officers charged with or suspected of involvement in serious violations of human rights and humanitarian law on UN peacekeeping assignments is another indicator of this culture of impunity. For instance, a Nepalese army officer serving with the UN peacekeeping operation in Sudan was arrested in January 2013 on charges of torture while visiting family in the UK. He was allegedly involved in the ill treatment of detainees while commander of the Gorusinge battalion barracks in Kapilbastu in 2005. Nepal's government strongly objected to the officer's arrest by UK police and called for his immediate release. Narayan Kaji Shrestha, the country's foreign minister, stated that the arrest was "against the general principle of international law and jurisdiction of a sovereign country".[196] The Torture Convention, to which both the UK and Nepal are parties, provides that a state must prosecute or extradite for prosecution a person found on its territory and alleged to have committed an act of torture or another act of serious ill treatment.[197] This obligation is an expression of the legal principle of universal jurisdiction, under which states have a duty to investigate international crimes regardless of where they took place.

The case of Major Niranjan Basnet provides another example of this culture of impunity.[198] Basnet was involved in the death in army custody of 15-year-old Maina Sunuwar. On 19 February 2004 Maina Sunuwar was taken from her home by a group of 15 uniformed soldiers to the Birendra Peace Operations Training Centre in Panchkhal, where she died following severe torture in the presence of seven army officers. In response to queries by her family, friends and others, the army first denied having arrested her and then stated she had been killed in an anti-terrorist operation. Under sustained pressure from the international community, the army initiated internal investigations and brought three officers before a court martial on 21 April 2004. According to army records, the three were sentenced to six months' imprisonment for minor offences of using improper interrogation techniques and not following procedures during the disposal of Maina Sunuwar's body.

As a result of continued pressure brought by Sunuwar's mother and human rights organizations, and following a Supreme Court directive in September 2007, the police brought murder charges against four army officers mentioned in the initial complaint filed by the victim's mother; but the four were not arrested. In September 2009 the district court in charge ordered the army to suspend immediately Major Niranjan Basnet, the only one of the four accused still serving, who had since been promoted from captain to major. Rather than suspending Basnet, the army ignored the court order and sent him on a UN peacekeeping assignment to Chad. In December 2009 the United Nations returned Basnet to Nepal after learning that he was charged with murder. Upon his arrival at the airport in Kathmandu, the army immediately took him into its custody and did not hand him over to the police. In January 2010 the UN Secretary-General urged the army to comply with the court order and suspend Basnet. Following internal army investigations, Basnet was found innocent. According to an army statement in July 2010, his return from the UN peacekeeping assignment violated international norms and regulations. At the time of writing, Major Basnet remains in army protection and has not been handed over to the police.

In addition to obstructing the establishment of effective external oversight and creating a pervasive culture of impunity for past crimes, efforts to promote *inclusion* in the security sector have been insufficient. Civil society groups, particularly victim groups, have not been given the opportunity to participate in SSR activities in any significant way. For instance, a national security policy was drafted and unilaterally adopted by a government committee without meaningful consultations. The policy itself was unspecific and did not address in any detail the most pressing security challenges of Nepal.[199] The army also rejected calls for transparency because, in its view, matters of military strategy and operations generally needed to be kept secret, contradicting international standards for information sharing and civilian oversight.[200] Family, friends and lawyers who sought information on the fate of victims and attempted to register complaints have often been threatened themselves.[201] The integration of former Maoist combatants into the army represented steps in the right direction. But the calls of historically marginalized groups such as the Dalits, Janajatis and Madeshis[202] for adequate representation in the army were not acted upon.[203]

Also, the army and other security actors have taken no significant steps to distance themselves from the abusive past in order to build their *legitimacy* and make themselves more trustworthy. In general terms, security institutions reiterated commitments to address the abusive past.[204] But whenever it came to specific abuses that occurred during the conflict, the army repeatedly held that its actions were justified and necessary to combat the enemy. For instance, in relation to Major Basnet, the chief of the army's legal department stated in July 2010 that "even going by the definition of the Military Act itself, it is clear that the army was acting against a common enemy then and functioning under the Terrorism and Disruptive Activities Act. Therefore, there is no case against Basnet."[205] On 8 October 2012 the OHCHR released the "Nepal Conflict Report", which analysed the most serious violations observed during the conflict between 1996 and 2006, and the Transitional Justice Reference Archive, a database with approximately 30,000 documents and cases.[206] But the government dismissed the report as "irrelevant".[207] The security and political elites of Nepal remained unapologetic about the past and maintained many of the policies they pursued during the conflict.

The failure to address conflict-era abuses effectively was not limited to the security sector but characteristic of the entire political establishment.[208] Successive governments headed by different political parties have authorized the withdrawal of criminal cases after having declared them politically motivated. More than 600 cases were withdrawn by just two cabinet decisions, one in October 2008 by a Maoist-led government and the other in November 2009 by a government led by the Communist Party of Nepal (Unified Marxist-Leninist). In November 2011 the government recommended a pardon for the only person convicted of a conflict-era crime.[209] The major political actors and groups sought to protect their own rather than to provide justice for conflict-era crimes. The failure to deal meaningfully with the abusive past manifested itself also in the continued delays of establishing a truth and reconciliation commission – at the time of writing it was more than six years since the armed conflict had ended – and in the flaws of the draft bill to create such a commission, particularly its amnesty provisions.[210]

In terms of victim support, the Interim Relief Program (IRP) was established in 2008 to give assistance to the victims of the conflict. By the end of 2012 it had provided benefits to over 30,000 conflict victims and approximately 80,000 internally displaced persons.[211] The implementation of the IRP represented an important achievement, providing material benefits to a significant number of victims. Yet it could not be qualified as a reparations programme and its benefits did not fully respond to the needs of the victims. Whereas relief "is the immediate assistance offered to those affected by man-made or natural disasters", reparations "recognize that rights have been violated and that the state is obligated to repair the consequences of the violation".[212] The benefits of the IRP did not represent reparations because its beneficiaries were not recognized as victims of human rights violations and it did not acknowledge the responsibility of the state for these violations. Again, the abusive past was not adequately addressed.

Nepal's failure to deal sincerely with its abusive past may have served the short-term interests of the security apparatus and related political elites. But it has also perpetuated the climate of impunity, creating the risk that the failure to hold security actors responsible for violations may spill over from the past into the present and impunity could become the norm of the future. Already, human rights organizations report ongoing violations in the post-conflict period by security actors who were not held accountable.[213] Abuses by security actors, impunity for past and present violations, the refusal to acknowledge past abuses and the failure to demonstrate a commitment to the rule of law continue to nourish distrust in the security sector. Moreover, Nepalese peacekeepers who are found to have been involved in past abuses while they serve in a peacekeeping operation not only harm the international standing of Nepal but also tarnish the image of the United Nations.

Not dealing with the abusive past has resulted in the continued exclusion of marginalized population groups from the security sector and the public sector in general. The ongoing denial of basic political, social and economic rights continues to consign these groups to marginalization and poverty, which constituted one of the root causes of the conflict.

Last but not least, the failure to address the abusive past has hampered the SSR process itself. Ignoring, justifying or downplaying past abuses and not seeing any wrong in the past meant that nothing had to change and democratization was not necessary after all. Not dealing with the abusive past not only violated domestic and international legal obligations by which Nepal is bound[214] and perpetuated impunity, exclusion and mistrust, but risked compromising the entire peace process and undermining the foundations of a democratic rule of law.

CONCLUSION

The analysis of the concepts of SSR and transitional justice in recent literature and policy documents reveals that the discourse between the two communities is limited and often marked by ignorance. In practice, DwP and SSR frequently share some of the same historical catalysts, face some of the same political challenges and target some of the same institutions, but apply different approaches, diverge in their immediate goals and contend for the same resources. As a result, both SSR and transitional justice are interested to pre-empt negative repercussions of the other's practices in their own programmes. The unavoidable interactions between the two fields remain at the level of competition and establish a relationship that is determined by defensive postures on both sides.

This paper argues that this situation is unsatisfactory. SSR and transitional justice are intrinsically related and can benefit from each other. On the one hand, DwP depends on SSR to prevent the recurrence of abuses in the future, which is a core element of justice in the aftermath of serious abuse. On the other hand, SSR can build a more effective, accountable and legitimate security sector if it deals with rather than ignores the legacies of an abusive past. Abusive histories of security institutions have detrimental effects on their functioning and may render SSR itself more difficult. In particular, abusive legacies often perpetuate a culture of impunity, extend the exclusion of marginalized population groups from the security sector and further erode the legitimacy of security actors, which undermines their effectiveness. The effects of abusive histories can be mitigated, in particular, by holistically strengthening accountability in the security sector, promoting the inclusion of all people, but especially victims and other marginalized groups, and proactively enhancing the legitimacy of security institutions.

The case of police reform in Bosnia and Herzegovina after Dayton indicates that ignoring legacies of past abuses can contribute to a continued pursuit of conflict-related goals and undermine the transition to the democratic rule of law. The case also reveals that dealing with an abusive past is difficult and tends to be resisted because it likely affects the situation of individuals in positions of power and it will, in some way or another, engage in acknowledging, undoing or reversing the outcomes of a conflict or of authoritarian rule and in compensating for the harm suffered. But whenever the abusive histories of the police were dealt with, the reform process made steps forward, police performance improved and public confidence in the police increased. The case also shows that adopting an exclusively forward-looking approach to SSR that is not interested in the past may initially appear an easier way out but will run into resistance whenever the promotion of the democratic rule of law affects the power bases of those involved in the conflict or the authoritarian regime.

This latest finding is also confirmed by the case of SSR in Nepal after 2006. The refusal by the army and related elites to acknowledge and deal with the abusive past reveals a lack of commitment to the norms of democratic governance which are at the core of the SSR concept. And in fact the army was not willing to accept external oversight mechanisms, refused to follow court orders and failed to hold abusive officers to account. Turning the page and devising a different future that is based on the democratic rule of law does not appear to be necessary if there was nothing wrong with the past in the first place.

To sum up in brief, this paper suggests the following.

- The current understanding of the relationship between SSR and transitional justice is inadequate and marked by misinterpretations, which leads to unhelpful competition between the two fields.
- A richer understanding of this relationship shows that DwP and SSR are intrinsically linked and can benefit from each other. Transitional justice depends on SSR to prevent the recurrence of abuses, which is a central component of justice in transition. SSR can better achieve its

own goals when it proactively deals with the abusive histories of security actors.

- Dealing with the past is not easy and will not be readily accepted. But ignoring abusive legacies risks extending the exclusion of marginalized groups, perpetuating cultures of impunity and further eroding public trust in the security sector. Not dealing with the abusive past also risks slowing down or even halting the SSR process itself and rendering more difficult the transition to a democratic rule of law.
- To deal effectively with abusive histories, SSR needs to pay particular attention to three aspects of reform.

  - ✓ First, SSR needs to promote the inclusion of marginalized groups by promoting their participation in SSR processes; advancing their representation in security institutions; establishing structures that meet the specific security needs of these groups; and empowering them as citizens.
  - ✓ Second, SSR needs to strengthen accountability for past, present and future abuses holistically by establishing multiple accountability mechanisms; providing accountability for past abuses by means of criminal prosecutions and vetting to exclude officers with abusive backgrounds; and developing the operational autonomy of security institutions to shield them from political interference.
  - ✓ Third, SSR needs to enhance the legitimacy of security institutions. The trustworthiness of these institutions is enhanced not only by actual reform measures that render the security sector more effective and accountable but also by targeted legitimacy-building measures that verbally or symbolically signal a turning away from the abusive past and reaffirm a commitment to the democratic rule of law.

Ignoring the effects of abusive histories or pretending that they do not exist does not eliminate them. SSR can be more effective when it deals head-on with abusive legacies in the sector rather than having to confront without preparation the consequences of an abusive past.

But addressing an abusive past is just one element of a comprehensive SSR approach, and a direct concern with this aspect by no means replaces mainstream approaches to SSR. Nevertheless, such a concern helps SSR to understand better the effects of an abusive past and draws attention to important areas of reform that are insufficiently considered in other SSR approaches.

The conversation between SSR and transitional justice actors has barely begun. Intensifying it, making serious efforts to understand each other and learning from each other can only be to the benefit of both DwP and SSR.

Empirical research on the relationship between SSR and transitional justice is limited. Further case-based research would be useful to understand this relationship better and clarify the interactions between the two fields. Such research could analyse the effects of both dealing and not dealing with the past in SSR. Also, the theses developed in this paper need to be further tested. Ideally, such research would be conducted jointly by transitional justice and SSR experts.

Vetting to exclude from security institutions officers with abusive backgrounds is of direct interest to both the SSR and the DwP communities. Vetting is a recurring theme in transitional settings. Examples include lustration processes in former communist countries, vetting the judiciary and police in Kenya and efforts to isolate politically representatives of former regimes in Iraq, Tunisia, Egypt and Libya. Vetting can be understood as an effort to provide accountability for past abuses. But primarily it aims at re-establishing civic trust and relegitimizing public institutions, and at disabling structures within which serious abuses were carried out in the past and which may destabilize the transition to a democratic rule of law.[215] The legal, human rights and transitional justice communities have been interested in the concept and conducted research on vetting,[216] but the SSR community has not paid much attention to the concept in transitional settings.[217] Joint research on vetting would provide a useful entry point to explore and develop the relationship between SSR and DwP.

Specific reform activities to deal with the abusive histories of security actors are proposed in this paper. Tensions between the SSR and transitional justice communities arise, however, not only over questions about whether or not to deal with the abusive past but also about when and in what order. Further case study research is needed to identify best practice in sequencing measures to deal with the past in SSR.

NOTES

[1] Transitional justice and dealing with the past are used interchangeably throughout this paper. In a recent issue of *Politorbis* (50(3), 2010), published by the Swiss Federal Department of Foreign Affairs, these two notions are also used interchangeably. On the origins and use of these notions see the subsection on "Preliminary descriptions".

[2] The 2011 mandate of the UN Support Mission in Libya (UNSMIL) provides a case in point. In Resolution 2009 the UN Security Council decided that two of UNSMIL's main areas of responsibility should be to support the restoration of public security and strengthening of accountable institutions, and to support transitional justice. United Nations, "The Situation in Libya", S/RES/2009, 16 September 2011, p. 3.

[3] The South African transition provided a notable exception to the antagonistic relationship between SSR and transitional justice. See, for instance, the work of the Center for the Study of Violence and Reconciliation, www.csvr.org.za.

[4] Erin Mobekk, "Transitional Justice and Security Sector Reform: Enabling Sustainable Peace", Occasional Paper 13, Geneva Centre for the Democratic Control of Armed Forces, Geneva, November 2006.

[5] Paul van Zyl, "Promoting Transitional Justice in Post-Conflict Societies", in Alan Bryden and Heiner Hänggi (eds), *Security Sector Governance in Post-Conflict Peacebuilding* (Münster: LIT Verlag, 2005, pp. 218–220).

[6] Tim Murithi, "The Role of Security Sector Reform in Dealing with the Past", *Politorbis*, 50(3), 2010, pp. 65–69.

[7] United Nations, "Securing Peace and Development: The Role of the United Nations in Supporting Security Sector Reform", Report of the Secretary-General, A/62/659-S/2008/39, 23 January 2008, p. 6.

[8] OECD DAC, *OECD DAC Handbook on Security System Reform (SSR): Supporting Security and Justice* (Paris: OECD, 2007, p. 21).

[9] DCAF ISSAT, *SSR in a Nutshell. Manual for Introductory Training on Security Sector Reform* (Geneva: DCAF/ISSAT, 2011, p. 5).

[10] Ibid.

[11] Clare Short, "Security Sector Reform and the Elimination of Poverty", speech, Centre for Defence Studies, King's College London, 9 March 1999, www.clareshort.co.uk/speeches/DFID/9%20March%201999.pdf.

[12] United Nations, note 7 above, pp. 3, 13.

[13] OECD DAC, note 8 above, pp. 13, 15.

[14] World Bank, *Conflict, Security, and Development. World Development Report 2011. Overview* (Washington, DC: World Bank, 2011, pp. 2, 5).

[15] For a detailed account of the origins of the concept of transitional justice see Paige Arthur, "How 'Transitions' Reshaped Human Rights: A Conceptual History of Transitional Justice", *Human Rights Quarterly*, 31, 2009, pp. 321–367.

[16] United Nations, "The Administration of Justice and the Human Rights of Detainees: Question of the Impunity of Perpetrators of Human Rights Violations (Civil and Political). Revised Final Report Prepared by Mr. Joinet", E/CN.4/Sub.2/1997/20/rev.1, 2 October 1997. These principles have been updated by Diane Orentlicher: United Nations, "Updated Set of Principles for the Protection and Promotion of Human Rights through

Action to Combat Impunity", E/CN.4/2005/102/Add. 1, 8 February 2005.

[17] United Nations, "The Rule of Law and Transitional Justice in Conflict and Post-Conflict Societies", Report of the Secretary-General, S/2004/616, 23 August 2004, p. 4.

[18] Ibid.

[19] Office of the High Commissioner for Human Rights, *Rule-of-Law Tools for Post-Conflict States. Prosecution Initiatives* (New York and Geneva: United Nations, 2006); Office of the High Commissioner for Human Rights, *Rule-of-Law Tools for Post-Conflict States. Maximizing the Legacy of Hybrid Courts* (New York and Geneva: United Nations, 2008).

[20] Office of the High Commissioner for Human Rights, *Rule-of-Law Tools for Post-Conflict States. Reparation Programmes* (New York and Geneva: United Nations, 2008).

[21] Office of the High Commissioner for Human Rights, *Rule-of-Law Tools for Post-Conflict States. Truth Commissions* (New York and Geneva: United Nations, 2006).

[22] International Center for Transitional Justice, "What Is Transitional Justice?", www.ictj.org. See also Louis Bickford, "Transitional Justice", in Dinah Shelton (ed.), *Encyclopedia of Genocide and Crimes against Humanity*, Vol. 3 (New York: Macmillan Reference, 2004, pp. 1045–1047); Office of the High Commissioner for Human Rights, *Rule-of-Law Tools for Post-Conflict States. Vetting: An Operational Framework* (New York and Geneva: United Nations, 2006).

[23] Pablo de Greiff provides a convincing and detailed account of how transitional justice measures are interlinked and aim to promote reconciliation and a democratic rule of law. See Pablo de Greiff, "A Normative Conception of Transitional Justice", *Politorbis*, 50(3), 2010, pp. 17–29.

[24] The report of the UN Secretary-General on rule of law and transitional justice provides definitions of the terms "rule of law", "justice", "administration of justice" and "transitional justice", and describes programmes to build and strengthen national justice systems. See United Nations, note 17 above, pp. 4, 12–13.

[25] See, for instance, the work of UN peacekeeping operations in the area of justice, www.un.org/en/peacekeeping/issues/ruleoflaw/justice.shtml.

[26] See, for instance, UN Development Programme, *Programming for Justice: Access for All* (Bangkok: UNDP, 2005), www.unrol.org/doc.aspx?d=2311.

[27] United Nations, note 17 above, p. 4.

[28] Examples include the adaption of the traditional *gacaca* system in Rwanda to hear genocide cases and the incorporation of elements of the *lisan* system in Timor-Leste in communal reconciliation processes. See notes 80 and 81 below. See also UN Rule of Law, "Informal Justice", www.un.org/en/peacekeeping/issues/ruleoflaw/justice.shtml.

[29] Timothy Garton Ash, "The Truth about Dictatorship", *New York Review of Books*, 19 February 1998, p. 35.

[30] Ibid., p. 40.

[31] See, for instance, issue 50(3), 2010, of the journal *Politorbis*, which is dedicated to the topic of "dealing with the past". On Switzerland's activities in the area of DwP see www.eda.admin.ch/eda/en/home/topics/peasec/peac/confre/depast.html.

[32] Mô Bleeker, "Preface", *Politorbis*, 50(3), 2010, pp. 7–9.

[33] See United Nations (2005), note 16 above, principles 19 and 24, pp. 12 and 14.

[34] de Greiff, note 23 above, p. 19.

35 Hence Heiner Hänggi looks at the specific SSR challenges in post-conflict contexts: Heiner Hänggi, "Establishing Security in Conflict-Ridden Societies: How to Reform the Security Sector", paper presented at Aspen European Strategy Forum, "International State-Building and Reconstruction Efforts – Experience Gained and Lessons Learned", Bonn, 18–21 September 2008, p. 10.

36 OECD DAC, note 8 above, p. 194. Transitional justice is, however, also described – albeit differently and not cross-referenced – as a separate post-conflict activity with which SSR is linked (p. 107).

37 Michael Brzoska, "Development Donors and the Concept of Security Sector Reform", Occasional Paper 4, Geneva Centre for the Democratic Control of Armed Forces, Geneva, November 2003, fn. 7.

38 See DFID, "Understanding and Supporting Security Sector Reform", 2002, www.dfid.gov.uk/pubs/files/supportingsecurity.pdf.

39 United Nations, note 7 above, except for a passing reference to the UN Secretary-General's report on the rule of law and transitional justice on p. 5.

40 United Nations, note 17 above, p. 4.

41 See DFID, "Justice and Accountability: A DFID Practice Paper", May 2008, http://webarchive.nationalarchives.gov.uk/+/http://www.dfid.gov.uk/Documents/public ations/briefing-justice-accountability.pdf.

42 For a detailed exploration of forward-looking justifications of accountability see Pablo de Greiff, "Deliberative Democracy and Punishment", *Buffalo Criminal Law Review*, 5(2), 2002, pp. 373–403.

43 de Greiff, note 23 above, p. 23.

44 United Nations (1997), note 16 above, p. 27.

45 See e.g. the list of guarantees of non-recurrence of violations in United Nations (2005), note 16 above, pp. 17–19.

46 See Elizabeth M. Cousens, "Introduction", in Elizabeth M. Cousens and Chetan Kumar (eds), *Peacebuilding as Politics: Cultivating Peace in Fragile Societies* (Boulder, CO: Lynne Rienner, 2001, p. 12). Cousens argues that "the most effective means to self-enforcing peace is to cultivate political processes and institutions that can manage group conflict without violence but with authority and, eventually, legitimacy".

47 United Nations, note 17 above.

48 Bickford, note 22 above, p. 1045.

49 International Center for Transitional Justice, note 22 above.

50 Hänggi, note 35 above, p. 10.

51 Heiner Hänggi, "Security Sector Reform", in Vincent Chetail (ed.), *Lexicon on Post-conflict Peacebuilding* (Oxford: Oxford University Press, 2007).

52 Hänggi, note 35 above, p. 14.

53 United Nations, note 7 above.

54 Ibid., p. 6.

55 United Nations, note 17 above.

56 See e.g. ibid., pp. 4, 11.

57 Ibid., pp. 4, 7, 11, 12, 14.

58 United Nations, note 7 above, pp. 7, 10, 13, 15.

59 Ibid., p. 3.

60   United Nations, note 17 above, pp. 3, 4 and 8 (stating that "prevention is the first imperative of justice" and referring to "prevention of wrongs" and "crime prevention").

61   Ibid., p. 11.

62   United Nations (2005), note 16 above, p. 17.

63   de Greiff, note 23 above, pp. 26–29, argues convincingly that the democratic rule of law is one of transitional justice's two final goals. Hänggi points out that democratic governance is one of two core elements of the SSR concept: Heiner Hänggi, "Conceptualising Security Sector Reform and Reconstruction", in Alan Bryden and Heiner Hänggi (eds), *Reform and Reconstruction of the Security Sector* (Geneva: DCAF, 2004, p. 5). See also Hänggi, note 51 above.

64   Pablo de Greiff, "Transitional Justice, Security, and Development. Security and Justice Thematic Paper", World Development Report 2011 Background Paper, World Bank, Washington, DC, 2010, pp. 8ff.

65   de Greiff, note 23 above, pp. 26–29.

66   Ibid., p. 18.

67   Hannah Arendt's distinction between, on the one hand, violence that is instrumental in character and uses tools to multiply natural strength, and, on the other, institutionalized power that enables a group to think and act and draws its legitimacy from the group is helpful here: "violence itself results in impotence. Where violence is no longer backed and restrained by power, the well-known reversal in reckoning with means and ends has taken place. The means, the means of destruction, now determine the end – with the consequence that the end will be the destruction of all power." Hannah Arendt, *On Violence* (Orlando, FL: Harcourt Brace, 1970, p. 54).

68   OECD DAC, note 8 above, p. 22.

69   Afghanistan Independent Human Rights Commission, "A Call for Justice: A Consultation on Past Human Rights Violations in Afghanistan", 2005, www.aihrc.org.af/media/files/Reports/Thematic reports/rep29_1_05call4justice.pdf.

70   Patrick Vinck, Phuong Pham, Suliman Baldo and Rachel Shigekane, "Living with Fear. A Population-based Survey on Attitudes about Peace, Justice, and Social Reconstruction in Eastern Democratic Republic of Congo", Berkeley-Tulane Initiative on Vulnerable Populations/International Center for Transitional Justice, August 2008, www.ictj.org/sites/default/files/ICTJ-DRC-Attitudes-Justice-2008-English.pdf.

71   Instance Equité et Réconciliation, "Rapport Final", 2005, www.ier.ma/rubrique.php3?id_rubrique=309.

72   OECD DAC, note 8 above, pp. 41–62.

73   Article 25(c) of the International Covenant on Civil and Political Rights provides that every citizen shall have the right to "have access, on general terms of equality, to public service in his country". See http://www2.ohchr.org/english/law/ccpr.htm.

74   United Nations, "Code of Conduct for Law Enforcement Officials", A/RES/34/169, 1979, Preamble, para. a, noting that "every law enforcement agency should be representative of and responsive and accountable to the community as a whole".

75   *Awareness Times*, "Sierra Leone Police Opens Gender Unit", *Awareness Times*, 21 June 2012, http://news.sl/drwebsite/publish/article_200520546.shtml.

76   For a comprehensive discussion of gender and SSR see Megan Bastik and Kristin Valasek (eds), *Gender and Security Sector Reform Toolkit* (Geneva: DCAF, 2008).

77 United Nations, "Report of the Secretary-General on the United Nations Mission in Bosnia and Herzegovina", S/2002/1314, 2002, p. 6, http://documents.un.org/. The achievements of this programme are, however, contested. Serious allegations have been raised about local police involvement in trafficking of women and girls, and about UN police officers visiting nightclubs as clients of trafficked women and girls. See Human Rights Watch, "Hopes Betrayed: Trafficking of Women and Girls to Post-Conflict Bosnia and Herzegovina for Forced Prostitution", 26 November 2002, www.unhcr.org/cgi-bin/texis/vtx/refworld/rwmain?page=printdoc&docid=3e31416f0.

78 UN Development Programme, "Mobile Courts Speed Up Justice in Somaliland", www.so.undp.org/index.php/Somalia-Stories/Mobile-courts-speed-up-justice-in-Somaliland.html.

79 Open Society Justice Initiative, "Fact Sheet: DRC Mobile Gender Courts", 19 July 2011, www.soros.org/publications/fact-sheet-democratic-republic-congo-mobile-gender-courts.

80 Penal Reform International has closely monitored and extensively reported on the *gacaca* process in Rwanda, www.penalreform.org/publications/gacaca-research-reports.

81 Amy Senier, "Traditional Justice as Transitional Justice: A Comparative Case Study of Rwanda and East Timor", *Praxis. The Fletcher Journal of Human Security*, 23, 2008, pp. 67–88.

82 Balkan Investigative Reporting Network, "Court Monitoring Annual Report 2012", January 2013, http://birn.eu.com/en/news-and-events/birn-presents-report-on-court-monitoring and http://birn.eu.com/en/file/show/birn%20raporti%20i%20monitorimit%20te%20gjykatave%202012-2013%20anglishtja.pdf.

83 For more information on CLARD see www.clardkosovo.org/.

84 UN Development Programme, "Afghan Women Escape Violence with Help of Legal Aid Center as Women's Livelihoods Improve", 10 April 2012, http://reliefweb.int/report/afghanistan/afghan-women-escape-violence-help-legal-aid-center-womens-livelihoods-improve.

85 UN Mission in Bosnia and Herzegovina, "Building a Better Future Together. December 1995–June 2002", www.un.org/Depts/DPKO/Missions/unmibh/Achiv.pdf.

86 Hansjörg Strohmeyer, "Collapse and Reconstruction of a Judicial System: The United Nations Missions in Kosovo and East Timor", *American Journal of International Law*, 95(46), 2001, p. 55.

87 More information on the work of the Liberia Media Center with its partners can be found at http://lmc.0fees.net/partners.html.

88 Free Press Unlimited, "Liberia Media Center Stands on Its Own Feet", 24 January 2013, https://www.freepressunlimited.org/en/article/liberia-media-center-stands-its-own-feet.

89 Avocats Sans Frontières, "Activities in Support of Access to Justice. An Overview", 2012, www.asf.be/wp-content/uploads/2012/10/AccèsJustice_2012_ENG.pdf.

90 OSCE Mission in Kosovo, "Background Report. Combatting Trafficking in Kosovo", 5 June 2001, www.osce.org/kosovo/13086.

91 David H. Bayley, "The Contemporary Practices of Policing: A Comparative View", paper presented at Center for Strategic and International Studies and Police Executive

Research Forum, 6 October 1997, quoted in C. E. Stone and H. H. Ward, "Democratic Policing: A Framework for Action", *Policing and Society*, 10(15), 2000, p. 15.

92　The UN principles to combat impunity recommend vetting to prevent the recurrence of abuses: United Nations (2005), note 16 above, principle 36, p. 18. The UN Secretary-General discusses vetting as an important component of transitional justice that facilitates the establishment of a stable rule of law in post-conflict countries: United Nations, note 17 above, pp. 17–18. The International Center for Transitional Justice supported the publication of an edited volume that includes several case studies and thematic chapters on transitional vetting: Alexander Mayer-Rieckh and Pablo de Greiff (eds), *Justice as Prevention: Vetting Public Employees in Transitional Societies* (New York: Social Science Research Council, 2007).

93　UN Human Rights Committee, "Concluding Observations of the Human Rights Committee: Guatemala, Considerations of Reports Submitted by State Parties under Article 40 of the Covenant", CCPR/CO/72/GTM, 2001, para. 13 (noting that "The perpetrators must be tried and punished: mere separation from service or dismissal from the army is not sufficient").

94　Office of the High Commissioner for Human Rights, note 19 above, pp. 9–10.

95　A more detailed description and basic guidelines to plan and implement a census and identification programme can be found in Arezou Azad, Alexander Mayer-Rieckh and Serge Rumin, "Census and Identification of Security Personnel after Conflict: A Tool for Practitioners", revised edn, International Center for Transitional Justice, 2009, http://ictj.org/publication/census-and-identification-security-personnel-after-conflict-tool-practitioners-revised.

96　Detailed guidelines to design and implement a vetting process after conflict can be found in Alexander Mayer-Rieckh, *Vetting Public Employees in Post-Conflict Settings: Operational Guidelines* (New York: UNDP Bureau for Crisis Prevention and Recovery, 2006).

97　See UNMIBH Human Rights Office, "From Joint to Unified Policing: Continuing Police Development in Central Bosnia", HRO 5/99 external, September 1999; UNMIBH Human Rights Office, "One City, One Police. Creating an Efficient, Impartial and Modern City Police Service in Mostar", HRO 2/00, December 2000 (copies on file).

98　de Greiff, note 23 above, p. 20.

99　General Balza said: "A minimal act of coming clean would be of little use if on reviewing the past we did not learn to avoid repeating it ever again in the future. Without searching out innovative terms, but rather appealing to longstanding military regulations, I take advantage of this opportunity to once again order the army, before the whole of society: no one is obliged to follow an immoral order or one that departs from the law or military regulations. The actions of those who do so are evil, worthy of the punishment its gravity requires. Without euphemisms, I say clearly: It is criminal to violate the National Constitution. It is criminal to issue immoral orders. It is criminal to obey immoral orders. It is criminal to use unjust and immoral means to achieve an end one believes is just ... We must no longer deny the horror experienced, and in this way think of our life as a society oriented toward the future, overcoming the shame and suffering."

100　General Balza's declaration is available (in Spanish) at http://memoriaviva5.

blogspot.com/2008/12/ declaracin-del-general-martn-balza.html.

[101] BBC, "Chile's Judges Apologise for Their Actions after Coup", BBC News, 4 September 2013, www.bbc.co.uk/news/world-latin-america-23967816.

[102] See the website of the museum, www.museodelamemoria.cl.

[103] See the website of Constitutional Hill, www.constitutionhill.org.za.

[104] *Süddeutsche Zeitung*, "Aufgeflogen nach 75 Jahren. Nazi-Spuren am Wiener Heldenplatz", *Süddeutsche Zeitung*, 20 July 2012, www.sueddeutsche.de/politik/wiener-heldenplatz-aufgeflogen-nach-jahren-1.1417384; *Der Standard*, "Deserteursdenkmal: Stadt prüft Heldenplatz", *Der Standard*, 20 April 2012, http://derstandard.at/1334795735003/Nationalsozialismus-Deserteursdenkmal-Stadt-prueft-Heldenplatz.

[105] See Pablo de Greiff, "The Role of Apologies in National Reconciliation Processes: On Making Trustworthy Institutions Trusted", in Mark Gibney, Rhoda E. Howard-Hassmann, Jean-Marc Coicaud and Niklaus Steiner (eds), *The Age of Apology: Facing Up to the Past* (Philadelphia, PA: University of Pennsylvania Press, 2008). On the importance of signalling see also World Bank, *Conflict, Security, and Development. World Development Report 2011* (Washington, DC: World Bank, 2011, pp. 19, 124–127).

[106] See the website of the museum, www.terrorhaza.hu.

[107] *New York Times*, "Stark History/Some See a Stunt: Memory Becomes Battleground in Budapest's House of Terror", *New York Times*, 2 August 2002, www.nytimes.com/2002/08/02/news/02iht-budapest_ed3_.html.

[108] The author was chief of the UNMIBH Human Rights Office from 1999 to 2001. The case study draws not only on experiences and sources gained during this period but subsequent field and desk research.

[109] The term "Bosniak" generally refers to those citizens of Bosnia and Herzegovina who have identified their nationality as Muslim.

[110] The census results can be found at www.fzs.ba.

[111] For an account of the conflicts in Yugoslavia see Laura Silber and Allan Little, *Yugoslavia: Death of a Nation*, revised edn (New York: TV Books, 1997). For a review of international intervention in Bosnia and Herzegovina see Elisabeth M. Cousens and Charles K. Carter, *Toward Peace in Bosnia. Implementing the Dayton Accords* (Boulder, CO: Lynne Rienner, 2001).

[112] Calculating the total number of conflict deaths remains controversial – early estimates put the number at more than 200,000. According to a 1994 UN report, the death toll exceeded 200,000: United Nations, "Final Report of the Commission of Experts Established Pursuant to Security Council Resolution 780 (1992)", S/1994/674, 27 May 1994, p. 84. The World Bank estimated in 1996 that some 250,000 people died or were missing: World Bank, *Bosnia and Herzegovina: Toward Economic Recovery* (Washington, DC: World Bank, 1996, p. 10). In a statement at the UN General Assembly in 2008, the head of the Bosnia and Herzegovina delegation said that according to the International Committee of the Red Cross, some 200,000 people had been killed including 12,000 children: United Nations, "Statement by Dr. Haris Silajdžić, Chairman of the Presidency of Bosnia and Herzegovina, Head of Delegation of Bosnia and Herzegovina, 63rd Session of the General Assembly", GA/10749, 23 September 2008, www.un.org/News/Press/docs/2008/ga10749.doc.htm. In 2010 the Demographic Unit at the Office of the Prosecutor of the International Criminal Tribunal for the former Yugoslavia concluded that the conflict

resulted in an estimated 104,732 casualties. Published by an independent Sarajevo-based research institute in 2013, *The Bosnian Book of the Dead* lists the names of 95,940 victims of the conflict and another 5,100 persons for whom the circumstances of death have yet to be established: Research and Documentation Centre, *The Bosnian Book of the Dead* (Sarajevo and Belgrade: IDC/HLC, 2013). The discrepancies in numbers are not only the result of calculation errors and political interests but also of differences in methodology and terminology.

[113] Of the around 2.2 million displaced, 1.2 million became refugees in 25 host countries and around 1 million were internally displaced within Bosnia and Herzegovina. See International Crisis Group, "Going Nowhere Fast. Refugees and Internally Displaced Persons in Bosnia and Herzegovina", Bosnia Report 23, ICG, Sarajevo, 1 May 1997, pp. 9–10.

[114] The Bosnian Croats established the so-called Croat Republic of Herceg Bosna in southern and western Herzegovina. The Bosnian Serbs established the autonomous Republika Srpska in northern and eastern Bosnia.

[115] The taking of Srebrenica stands as the most severe atrocity of the conflict. An estimated 7,000 Muslim men were massacred by Serb forces, while the United Nations, European nations and the United States stood passively by. See David Rhode, *Endgame: The Betrayal and Fall of Srebrenica, Europe's Worst Massacre since World War II* (New York: Farrar, Strauss and Giroux, 1997); United Nations, "Report of the Secretary-General Pursuant to General Assembly Resolution 53/35. The Fall of Srebrenica", A/54/549, 15 November 1999.

[116] The Washington Agreement of 1 March 1994 was brokered by the US government. For the text see www.usip.org/library/pa/bosnia/washagree_03011994_toc.html.

[117] "General Framework Agreement for Peace in Bosnia and Herzegovina", 14 December 1995, in Office of the High Representative, *Bosnia and Herzegovina. Essential Texts*, 2nd edn (Sarajevo: Office of the High Representative, 1998, pp. 16–52); hereinafter Dayton Peace Agreement.

[118] Cousens and Carter, note 111 above, p. 26.

[119] Dayton Peace Agreement, note 117 above, Annex 4, Constitution.

[120] Washington Agreement, note 116 above, Article II.

[121] Dayton Peace Agreement, note 117 above, Annex 4, Constitution, Article III. Over the following years the high representative imposed the creation of several state-level rule of law institutions, in particular the State Border Service, the State Information and Protection Agency, and the State Court.

[122] Washington Agreement, note 116 above, Article III.

[123] Dayton Peace Agreement, note 117 above, Annex 4; Constitution of Bosnia and Herzegovina, Article III, para. 2(c) and Annex 11; Agreement on the International Police Task Force, Article I, para. 1.

[124] Dayton Peace Agreement, note 117 above, Annex 7, Article I, para. 3(e).

[125] Ibid., Annex 11, Article I, para. 2.

[126] United Nations, "Establishment of a UN Civilian Police Force to Be Known as the International Police Task Force (IPTF) and a UN Civilian Office for the Implementation of the Peace Agreement for Bosnia and Herzegovina", S/RES/1035, 21 December 1995.

127 United Nations, "Report of the Secretary-General Pursuant to Security Council Resolution 1026 (1995)", S/1995/1031, 13 December 1995, pp. 7–8.

128 United Nations, *The Blue Helmets: A Review of United Nations Peacekeeping*, 3rd edn (New York: United Nations, 1996, p. 563).

129 Dayton Peace Agreement, note 117 above, Annex 11, Article III, para. 1.

130 United Nations, "The Situation in Bosnia and Herzegovina", S/RES/1088, 12 December 1996.

131 See Andrew F. Tully, "Kosova and Bosnia: A Tale of Two Police Forces", RFE/RL Balkan Report 5(64), 11 September 2001, www.rferl.org/content/article/1341157.html.

132 These figures are based on estimates made by the UN police reconnaissance mission that travelled to Bosnia and Herzegovina in November 1995. See United Nations, note 127 above, p. 7. Other sources estimated even higher numbers. The special rapporteur of the UN Commission on Human Rights indicated that the estimated number of police officers in the Republika Srpska alone could be as high as 50,000: Elisabeth Rehn, "Report on the Human Rights Situation in Bosnia and Herzegovina", CHR, 54th Session, E/CN.4/1998/13, 15 October 1997, para. 118.

133 According to the last official census in 1991, Bosnia and Herzegovina had a population of 4,377,000. These numbers dropped to below 4 million inhabitants after the conflict but no official figures were available.

134 United Nations, "Twelfth United Nations Congress on Crime Prevention and Criminal Justice", A/CONF.213/3, 1 February 2010, p. 19.

135 Eurostat, "Police Officers", http://appsso.eurostat.ec.europa.eu/nui/show.do?dataset= crim_plce&lang=en.

136 International Crisis Group, "War Criminals in Bosnia's Republika Srpska. Who Are the People in Your Neighbourhood?", Balkans Report 103, 2 November 2000, www.crisisgroup.org/~/media/Files/europe/Bosnia%2039.pdf.

137 "Agreement on Restructuring the Police Federation of Bosnia and Herzegovina", 25 April 1996, in Office of the High Representative, *Bosnia and Herzegovina. Essential Texts*, 2nd edn (Sarajevo: Office of the High Representative, 1998, pp. 81–83).

138 The information on Stolac is based on internal UNMIBH reports on file with the author.

139 See the statement of Kelly Moore, UNMIBH spokesperson, at the joint press conference, 11 March 1999, www.nato.int/sfor/trans/1999/t990311a.htm.

140 The Ustasha was a fiercely nationalist, fanatically Catholic and fascist movement founded in the 1930s to create an independent Croatian state. Ante Pavelic was its leader. In 1941 it was designated by Nazi Germany to rule the Independent State of Croatia. The Ustasha was chiefly responsible for executing the Holocaust in its territories and for the deaths of hundreds of thousands of non-Croatian Yugoslav citizens. With the German and Italian occupation forces, it fought an increasingly unsuccessful campaign against the Yugoslav partisans. The Ustasha state crumbled with the withdrawal of the German forces in 1944–1945.

141 Dayton Peace Agreement, note 117 above, Annex 11, Article I, para. 1.

142 "Framework Agreement on Police Restructuring, Reform and Democratisation in the Republika Srpska", 9 December 1998; hereinafter RS Framework Agreement. The agreement was signed in Banja Luka by Republika Srpska government and UNMIBH

representatives, following extremely difficult and protracted negotiations with Republika Srpska authorities (copy on file).

[143] International Crisis Group, "Policing the Police in Bosnia: A Further Reform Agenda", Balkans Report 130, 10 May 2002, pp. 39–42, www.crisisgroup.org/~/media/Files/europe/Bosnia%2046.pdf.

[144] Ibid.

[145] United Nations, "Report of the Secretary-General on the United Nations Mission in Bosnia and Herzegovina", S/2002/1314, 2002, pp. 4–5, http://documents.un.org/.

[146] UNMIBH Human Rights Office (1999, 2000), note 97 above.

[147] UN Mission in Bosnia and Herzegovina, note 85 above.

[148] On registration processes as a means to establish accountability see Azad et al., note 95 above.

[149] Alexander Mayer-Rieckh, "Vetting to Prevent Future Abuses: Reforming the Police, Courts and Prosecutor's Offices in Bosnia and Herzegovina", in Mayer-Rieckh and de Greiff, note 92 above, pp. 180–220; Gregory L. Naarden, "Non-Prosecutorial Sanctions for Grave Violations of International Humanitarian Law: Wartime Conduct of Bosnian Police Officials", *American Journal of International Law*, 97, 2003, pp. 342–352.

[150] United Nations, note 145 above, pp. 3–4.

[151] Mayer-Rieckh, note 149 above, p. 189.

[152] For more information on the establishment of police commissioners see United Nations, note 145 above, pp. 1, 4; see also International Crisis Group, note 143 above, pp. 33–36.

[153] Office of the High Representative, "Decision on the Use of Inoffensive Insignia and Symbols by the Police and Judicial Institutions in the Federation", 30 July 1999, www.ohr.int/decisions/plipdec/default.asp?content_id=178.

[154] UNMIBH, "Statement by the Special Representative of the Secretary-General, Jacques Paul Klein, on the Continued Use of Non-Neutral and Offensive Insignia by Police and Judicial Institutions", Press Release #63-(99), 21 December 1999 (copy on file).

[155] UNMIBH Human Rights Office, internal reports (copies on file).

[156] In 2000 confidence expressed in the police was between 46.2 per cent and 73.3 per cent; in 2003 it was between 63.2 per cent and 79.0 per cent. UNDP Early Warning System in Bosnia and Herzegovina, "Annual Report 2000", pp. 16–17, and "Annual Report 2003", pp. 15–16, www.ews.undp.ba/eng/izvjestaji.asp.

[157] UNMIBH Human Rights Office, internal reports (copies on file). Lack of security was usually cited as one of the reasons for minorities not to return to their places of origin. The percentage of those believing there is a significant level of corruption in the police remained roughly the same. See UNDP Early Warning System in Bosnia and Herzegovina (2000), ibid., p. 17; UNDP Early Warning System in Bosnia and Herzegovina (2003), ibid., pp. 15–16.

[158] International Crisis Group, note 143 above, p. ii.

[159] Charles Call, quoted in Cousens and Carter, note 111 above, p. 61, endnote 39. See also Gemma Collantes Celador, "Police Reform: Peacebuilding Through 'Democratic Policing'?", *International Peacekeeping*, 12(3), 2005, pp. 364–376.

[160] For a pronounced position on this issue see European Stability Initiative, "Travails of the European Raj", 3 July 2003, www.esiweb.org/index.php?lang=en&id=156&document_ID=59. But see also International Crisis Group, "Bosnia's Nationalist Governments: Paddy

Ashdown and the Paradoxes of State Building", Balkans Report 146, 22 July 2003, www.crisisgroup.org/en/regions/europe/balkans/bosnia-herzegovina/146-bosnias-nationalist-governments-paddy-ashdown-and-the-paradoxes-of-state-building.aspx.

[161] Laurie Nathan, *No Ownership, No Commitment: A Guide to Local Ownership of Security Sector Reform* (Birmingham: University of Birmingham, 2007, p. 1).

[162] European Stability Initiative, "On Mount Olympus. How the UN Violated Human Rights in Bosnia and Herzegovina, and Why Nothing Has Been Done to Correct It", 10 February 2007, www.esiweb.org/pdf/esi_document_id_84.pdf.

[163] From the outset the mission was heralded as "police reform by police officers". See International Crisis Group, "Bosnia's Stalled Police Reform: No Progress, no EU", Europe Report 164, 6 September 2005, p. 13, www.crisisgroup.org/en/regions/europe/balkans/bosnia-herzegovina/164-bosnias-stalled-police-reform-no-progress-no-eu.aspx. See also Alexander Mayer-Rieckh, "Time to Be More Serious about Post-Conflict Police Development", *Sicherheit und Frieden. Security and Peace*, 28(2), 2010, pp. 81–88.

[164] In 2005 the International Crisis Group concluded that "no matter what criteria are used to assess EUPM performance, the indicators are depressing": International Crisis Group, ibid., p. 12.

[165] This case study is based on desk research and covers the period from 2006 to 2012. In part the study draws on Alexander Mayer-Rieckh, "Building Trust and Strengthening the Rule of Law. Vetting the Security Sector in Nepal", ICTJ Briefing, April 2012, http://ictj.org/publications.

[166] There were 125 ethnic groups reported in the 2011 census. Chetri is the largest ethnic group with 16.6 per cent of the total population, followed by Brahman-Hill (12.2 per cent), Magar (7.1 per cent), Tharu (6.6 per cent), Tamang (5.5 per cent) and Newar (5.0 per cent). See Government of Nepal, National Planning Commission Secretariat, Central Bureau of Statistics, "National Population and Housing Census 2011 (National Report)", November 2012, http://cbs.gov.np/wp-content/uploads/2012/11/National%20 Report.pdf.

[167] World Bank, "Unequal Citizens: Gender, Caste and Ethnic Exclusion in Nepal", 2006, www-wds.worldbank.org/external/default/WDSContentServer/WDSP/IB/2006/12/05/ 000090341_20061205151859/Rendered/PDF/379660Nepal0GSEA0Summary0Report01P UBLIC1.pdf. Together, the Dalits and the Janajatis constitute more than half of Nepal's population, but the Dalits own less than 1 per cent of the land and earn 80 per cent less than the average Nepali. See also Rajeev Goyal, Puja Dhawan and Smita Narula, "The Missing Piece of the Puzzle: Caste Discrimination and the Conflict in Nepal", NYU Center for Human Rights and Global Justice, New York, 2005, www.chrgj.org/docs/Missing%20 Piece%20of%20the%20Puzzle.pdf.

[168] The Nepal Police has recorded 1,485 police personnel who "attained martyrdom fearlessly fighting the terrorists". See Nepal Police, "Tribute to Martyrs", www.nepalpolice.gov.np/ index.

[169] Bishnu Raj Upreti and Peter Vanhoutte, "Security Sector Reform in Nepal: Challenges and Opportunities", in Hans Born and Albrecht Schnabel (eds), *Security Sector Reform in Challenging Environments* (Münster: LIT Verlag, 2009, p. 170).

[170] Office of the UN High Commissioner for Human Rights, "Nepal Conflict Report", October 2012, pp. 58–60, www.ohchr.org/EN/Countries/AsiaRegion/Pages/NepalConflict Report.aspx.

[171] The Informal Sector Service Centre (INSEC), a leading human rights organization in Nepal, recorded 13,236 people killed. See INSEC, "Conflict Victim Profile", August 2010, www.insec.org.np/victim/. According to the International Committee of the Red Cross, more than 1,350 individuals who went missing during the conflict remain unaccounted for: International Committee of the Red Cross, "Nepal: Red Cross Releases Documentary on Conflict-related Missing", 8 August 2010, www.icrc.org/web/eng/siteeng0.nsf/html/nepal-news-060810. According to the Ministry for Peace and Reconstruction, a government task force established that the conflict led to at least 17,265 deaths and 1,327 disappearances: Nepal Monitor, "Recording Nepal Conflict: Victims in Numbers", 23 July 2011, www.nepalmonitor.com/2011/07/recording_nepal_conf.html. These figures do not separate lawful and unlawful killings.

[172] Office of the UN High Commissioner for Human Rights, note 170 above. Amnesty International estimates that at least half of the state victims were killed unlawfully: Amnesty International, "Nepal: A Deepening Human Rights Crisis", Amnesty International, London, 19 December 2002, p. 1.

[173] The CPA contains parallel commitments to integrate and rehabilitate the Maoist fighters, and to democratize and downsize the Nepal Army. See "Comprehensive Peace Agreement concluded between the Government of Nepal and the Communist Party of Nepal (Maoist)", 21 November 2006, para. 4. See also "The Interim Constitution of Nepal", 2063 (2007), Article 144(3)–(4).

[174] For a more detailed account of early SSR efforts see Upreti and Vanhoutte, note 169 above, pp. 165–187.

[175] Ibid., p. 168.

[176] The so-called Seven Point Agreement of 1 November 2011. An unofficial translation of the agreement can be found at www.southasiaanalysis.org/%5Cnotes7%5Cnote 639.html.

[177] Advocacy Forum and Redress, "Held to Account. Making the Law Work to Fight Impunity in Nepal", Advocacy Forum, Kathmandu, and Redress, London, December 2011, pp. 14, 23–26.

[178] International Crisis Group, "Nepal: From Two Armies to One", Asia Report 211, ICG, Kathmandu and Brussels, 18 August 2011.

[179] Advocacy Forum and Redress, note 177 above, p. 29.

[180] Lisa Ibscher, "Challenges in Implementing the Peace Agreement in Nepal: Dealing with the Impasse", *Politorbis*, 50(3), 2010, p. 187.

[181] Ibid., pp. 185–187.

[182] Peace Secretariat of the Government of Nepal, "Agreements and Understandings on Peace Negotiation of Nepal", Government of Nepal, Kathmandu, 2007, p. 3, www.ncf.org.np/upload/files/775_en_cover%20and%20con.pdf.

[183] "Comprehensive Peace Agreement", note 173 above, para. 5.2.5.

[184] "Interim Constitution of Nepal", note 173 above, Articles 32 (right to constitutional remedy) and 107 (jurisdiction of the Supreme Court). See also Article 8 of the Universal

Declaration of Human Rights and Article 2 of the International Covenant on Civil and Political Rights.

[185] "His Majesty's Government's Commitment on the Implementation of Human Rights and International Humanitarian Law", announced by Prime Minister Surya Bahadur Thapa, 26 March 2004 (unofficial translation), p. 3, www.mofa.gov.np/uploads/files/news/20060310120720.pdf.

[186] Office of the UN High Commissioner for Human Rights, note 170 above, pp. 177–178.

[187] Ibid., pp. 178–179.

[188] Ibid., fn. 813.

[189] Advocacy Forum and Redress, note 177 above, p. 15.

[190] International Crisis Group, "Crisis Watch", No. 112, 1 December 2012, www.crisisgroup.org/~/media/Files/CrisisWatch/2012/cw112.ashx.

[191] Advocacy Forum and Redress, note 177 above, p. 16.

[192] Advocacy Forum and Human Rights Watch, "Nepal: Adding Insult to Injury. Continued Impunity for Wartime Abuses", Advocacy Forum, Kathmandu, and Human Rights Watch, New York, December 2011, pp. 14–17.

[193] Office of the UN High Commissioner for Human Rights in Nepal, "OHCHR Calls for Comprehensive Human Rights Vetting as Part of the Peace Process", press release, 28 August 2009, http://nepal.ohchr.org/en/resources/Documents/English/pressreleases/Year%202009/August2009/2009_08_28_PR_Meeting_withCoAS_E.pdf; Mayer-Rieckh, note 165 above.

[194] For certain serious crimes, international law places an obligation on states either to extradite or to prosecute (*aut dedere aut iudicare*). Amnesties for such crimes are therefore prohibited. They include, in particular, genocide, crimes against humanity, extrajudicial executions, enforced disappearance, torture and slavery. See United Nations (2005), note 16 above, principles 19 and 24, pp. 12 and 14.

[195] Kamal Raj Sigdel, "Transitional Justice: Parties Go for Blanket Amnesties", 17 December 2011, www.ekantipur.com/2011/12/17/top-story/transitional-justice-parties-go-for-blanket-amnesty/345662.html.

[196] BBC, "Nepal's Colonel Kumar Lama Charged in UK with Torture", BBC News, 5 January 2013, www.bbc.co.uk/news/world-asia-20914282.

[197] Convention against Torture and Other Cruel, Inhuman and Degrading Treatment or Punishment, Article 7. Accordingly, section 134 of the UK's Criminal Justice Act defines torture as a universal jurisdiction crime.

[198] On the Basnet case see Advocacy Forum, "Maina Sunuwar. Separating Fact from Fiction", Advocacy Forum, Kathmandu, 2010; Office of the UN High Commissioner for Human Rights, note 170 above, p. 24; Advocacy Forum and Human Rights Watch, "Waiting for Justice. Unpunished Crimes from Nepal's Armed Conflict", Advocacy Forum, Kathmandu, and Human Rights Watch, New York, September 2008, pp. 33ff; Advocacy Forum and Human Rights Watch, note 192 above, pp. 17–19; Advocacy Forum and Redress, note 177 above, pp. 14–15; Al Jazeera, "Nepal Pressured to Arrest War Criminals", 16 January 2013, www.youtube.com/watch?v=SovcDeit1C4.

[199] International Crisis Group, note 178 above, p. 23.

[200] International Crisis Group, "Nepal's Fitful Peace Process", Asia Briefing 120, ICG, Kaathmandu and Brussels, 7 April 2011, p. 17.

201 See, for instance, Advocacy Forum and Human Rights Watch, note 192 above, pp. 17, 30.

202 The Madeshis are the population groups based in the Madesh, the plains of southern Nepal bordering India.

203 Upreti and Vanhoutte, note 169 above, p. 178; International Crisis Group, note 200 above, pp. 17–18; International Crisis Group, note 178 above, p. 23.

204 Office of the UN High Commissioner for Human Rights, note 170 above, pp. 178–179.

205 Akanshya Shah, "Army Gives Basnet Clean Chit, Claims UN Violated Norms", South Asians for Human Rights, 14 July 2010, www.southasianrights.org/?p=1233.

206 Office of the UN High Commissioner for Human Rights, note 170 above. The Transitional Justice Reference Archive is available at http://nepalconflictreport.ohchr.org.

207 International Crisis Group, note 190 above.

208 International Crisis Group, "Nepal's Peace Process: The Endgame Nears", Asia Briefing 131, 13 December 2011, pp. 14–16.

209 Advocacy Forum and Redress, note 177 above, pp. 12–13.

210 Initially, the establishment of two commissions was envisaged: a truth and reconciliation commission and a commission of inquiry on the disappearance of persons. For the history of truth-seeking in post-conflict Nepal and options forward see Eduardo González Cueva, "Seeking Options for the Right to Truth in Nepal", ICTJ Briefing, November 2012, http://ictj.org/sites/default/files/ICTJ-Briefing-Paper-Nepal-Ordinance-Dec-2012-ENG.pdf.

211 Ruben Carranza, "Relief, Reparations, and the Root Causes of Conflict in Nepal", International Center for Transitional Justice, New York, October 2012, p. 1.

212 Ibid., p. 5.

213 Advocacy Forum and Human Rights Watch, note 192 above, fn. 1 and pp. 22–24.

214 Human Rights Committee, "General Comment No. 31, Nature of the General Legal Obligation on States Parties to the Covenant", CCPR/C/21/Rev.1/Add.13, 29 March 2004, p. 6.

215 Mayer-Rieckh, note 96 above, p. 9.

216 See, for instance, Parliamentary Assembly of the Council of Europe, "Measures to Dismantle the Heritage of Former Communist Totalitarian Systems", Resolution 1096 (1996), adopted 26 June 1996, Council of Europe, Strasbourg; Inter-American Court on Human Rights, "Velásquez Rodríguez Case", OAS/ser. L/V/III. 19, Doc. 13, App. VI, 1988, pp. 174–175; Roman Boed, "An Evaluation of the Legality and Efficacy of Lustration as a Tool of Transitional Justice", *Columbia Journal of Transitional Law*, 37, 1999, pp. 357–402; Federico Andreu-Guzmán, "Due Process and Vetting", in Mayer-Rieckh and de Greiff, note 92 above, pp. 448–481; Herman Schwartz, "Lustration in Eastern Europe", *Parker School of East European Law Journal*, 1(2), 1994, pp. 141–171.

217 In the SSR context the term "vetting" usually refers to a screening process to clear candidates for sensitive public office positions. Such vetting processes are used in stable contexts to exclude individuals who represent a threat to state security or carry an increased risk of abuse of power. See, for instance, Geneva Centre for the Democratic Control of Armed Forces, "Vetting and the Security Sector", DCAF Backgrounder Series, Geneva, 2006.

www.ingramcontent.com/pod-product-compliance
Lightning Source LLC
Chambersburg PA
CBHW080500030726
47592CB00011B/3198